Before and After

Born in Bayswater in 1875, Edith Morley 'did hate being a girl', though she found the middle-class conventions of the day restrictive rather than repressive and benefited from a good education, thanks to her surgeon-dentist father and well-read mother. She obtained an 'equivalent' degree from Oxford University (the only type available to the few female students at the time) and was appointed Professor of English Language at University College, Reading, in 1908, becoming the first female professor in the United Kingdom. She is best known as the primary twentieth-century editor of Henry Crabb Robinson's writings (the author of a comprehensive biography) and for her *Women Workers in Seven Professions: A Survey of their Economic Conditions and Prospects* (1914), published while she was a member of the Fabian Executive Committee. *Before and After*, written after her retirement in 1940, was 'intended to relate my experiences to the background of my period and to portray incidents in the life of a woman born in the last quarter of the nineteenth century'. She was awarded an OBE in 1950 for her work in setting up the Reading Refugee Committee and assisting Jewish refugees in World War II. She died in 1964.

D1147445

Also published by Two Rivers Press:

Before and After

Reminiscences of a working life

by Edith Morley

edited by Barbara Morris

TWO
RIVERS
PRESS

University of
Reading

First published in the UK in 2016 by Two Rivers Press
7 Denmark Road, Reading RG1 5PA.
www.tworiverspress.com

ISBN 978-1-909747-16-6 (pb) | 978-1-909747-19-7 (hb)

1 2 3 4 5 6 7 8 9

Two Rivers Press is represented in the UK by Inpress Ltd
and distributed by Central Books.

Cover and text design by Nadja Guggi
Typeset in Janson and Parisine

Printed and bound in Great Britain by Ashford Colour Press, Gosport.

Acknowledgements
Two Rivers Press would like to thank the Friends of Reading University and
the Reading University Women's Club for their financial support of this project.
We are also grateful to the previous and current Heads of the Department
of English Literature, in the School of Literature and Languages, for their help
in coordinating the various sources of support for this project both inside
and outside the University of Reading.

I have been very glad to pay for
the production and initial printings
of this Edith Morley memoir
as a donation to the English Literature Department
of the University of Reading

in ever loving memory of my late wife,
Ann Patricia Palmer née Newton (1938–2011),

who was an undergraduate, leading to her BA degree,
in that Department during 1956 to 1959,
and whose consequential, continued enthusiasm
for English literature
was of great benefit to Ann, and to me as a scientist,
throughout the forty-nine wonderful years of our marriage.

—*Derek W. Palmer*

Contents

Foreword

Every woman now working in British universities – or in any other profession, for that matter – will recognise Edith Morley's story, told in this wonderfully direct memoir. The first woman to be a 'professor' in the United Kingdom, she was as 'awkward', 'difficult' and 'determined' as any of her twenty-first century successors must be (and we are still described in the same way). Quite simply, she took on the establishment, as feminists have done ever since.

When the first professors at the new University College at Reading were designated in 1907, Morley was left off the list of those honoured. Her description of the controversy is instantly recognisable, even now. She thought that her achievements were not quite up to the honour of a chair; but when she realised that she was the only 'lecturer in charge of a subject' who was not to be made professor, she took a certain fire in her soul – and refused to stay in her post unless she was 'promoted'.

It remains a credit to the new University at Reading that it broke convention and gave Morley a chair. It is perhaps even more of a credit to Morley herself that she stood up to those conventions and claimed the recognition due to her. She would no doubt be disheartened to discover that – more than a century later – her female successors in the academy are still sometimes struggling to win their due rewards.

Professor Mary Beard
January 2016

Introduction

The University of Reading reaches its 90th birthday in 2016, and the publication of Edith Morley's memoir, *Before and After*, is part of the celebration, for Morley was involved at the start of the University's life and provides a very personal account of its growth and teething troubles. The struggles she was engaged in to become the first female professor in the country were considerable and are no less relevant today, but she must have influenced opinion and practices in the University, because in 1933 women made up roughly one-fifth of the full-time academic staff in the three Faculties. When an enquiry came from the Vice-Chancellor at Liverpool about the situation when women married, Sibly, Reading's Vice-Chancellor, simply indicated that there had been no problem or questions raised when five of the female staff got married: 'Reading had come quite easily to accept matters of which other universities made very heavy weather indeed'.[*]

Morley wrote her reminiscences after her retirement in 1940. The typescript exists in three copies in the Morley archive held in the University of Reading's Special Collections. One of these copies has been heavily annotated with manuscript additions in her small but neat writing, and this copy has formed the present text.

In 1944 she sent it to the publishers Allen and Unwin who rejected it on the grounds that 'those who don't remember these things will have read of them often enough in novels of the period' and that it was 'for yesterday or tomorrow, but not today'. Given the wartime restrictions on paper, publishers were very limited in what they could take on, and they were probably right to refuse it. But 'tomorrow' is now, and a good time to make available this memoir. What was still familiar to potential readers in 1944 is now no longer so, and her descriptions of her life growing up in the last quarter of the nineteenth century are fascinating, while her account of the 1938 refugee crisis has many resonances for today.

She wrote the memoir partly to explain to young people what life was like for young women of her generation and class, and partly to chronicle her involvement in the issues of the time – more particularly, early feminist and socialist thinking and activities – and the people she met who were involved in them. She omits many aspects of her life: she was born into a Jewish family but never mentions religion or how it might have affected her growing up. And, perhaps more strangely, she mentions nothing of her major literary activity, the editing of the works of the prolific eighteenth-century diarist and journalist Henry Crabb Robinson.

Rejected by the publisher, her text was never edited, and had she been able to publish, I think she would have made many amendments. We have however been anxious to present her text as closely as possible to the one she wrote in 1944. Editing a posthumous work brings problems and responsibilities, as there is no possibility of consulting the author. We have shortened the title which in the original was 'Looking before and after'. I have provided additional punctuation, and have made minimal orthographic changes in line with contemporary practice. Occasional sentences were convoluted and have been straightened out. Morley's memory was not always reliable, and a few factual errors have been quietly corrected. Morley introduced several footnotes which are marked with * and †. In addition to her these, I have supplied, where possible, explanations of some of her more obscure references as numbered footnotes. Morley mentions very many people, some familiar, others less so, and the latter are also briefly described, singly or collectively, in the footnotes. For those people who most exemplify her main concerns – feminists, Fabians, academics, and people associated with Reading University – brief biographies are provided at the back of the book and set in small caps. The very famous require no comment.

What was she like as a person? Holt describes her thus: 'She was provocative, disturbing, aggressive, and intransigent: others kept their distance to avoid collision and damage. ... Yet she loved humanity… . She was ever ready to fight for the oppressed, especially if feminine'.[*] Her obituary in the local paper says, 'She fought not only with courage but sometimes aggression and always with passionate sincerity for Human Rights and freedom'.[†]

The publication of these memoirs would not have been possible without the generous donation made by Derek Palmer, in memory of his late wife Ann, an undergraduate in the English Department in the late 1950s. I am also very grateful to the staff of the Special Collections Department, and to Professor Peter Robinson and Anke Ueberberg for their advice and support.

Barbara Morris

[*]   J.C. Holt, *The University of Reading: The first fifty years* (Reading University Press, 1977)

[†]   *Reading Mercury*, 23rd January 1964

To my former colleagues and students,
in gratitude

Preface

This book is not an autobiography. It is intended to relate my experiences to the background of my period and to portray incidents in the life of a woman born in the last quarter of the nineteenth century. My youth was passed in conditions not always realised by the young people of today. Later on my work and interests brought me into contact with various movements and persons of historic importance, and now the enforced leisure of advancing years gives me the opportunity to indulge in the reminiscent mood, which is the prerogative of age, and to set down some records of the past for the benefit of present-day readers.

Edith Morley

CHAPTER I:

Childhood background

I was born in 1875, in the tall Bayswater house which was to be my home until my mother's death in 1926. My father was a surgeon-dentist with a West End practice, and since he had six children, the eldest an invalid, there was never much money to spare for luxuries. On the other hand, since he was a great stickler for professional etiquette and the proprieties, we were brought up strictly in accordance with the middle-class conventions of the day, which included, happily, a beloved nurse and as good an education as could be managed for all of us, a six-weeks country or seaside holiday every summer and regular visits to the pantomime or theatre at Christmas or on birthdays. Certainly in my own home and in the houses we visited, nothing was known of the Victorian suppression and repression of children about which so much is read today. On the contrary, I was myself a much indulged and very spoiled little girl, very conscious of my importance as the only sister among four brothers, two much older, one near my own age, and one nine years younger. But I did hate being a girl[*] and can still remember my indignation at hearing my brother told that only girls cheated at games and the like, or cried when they were hurt. And how I hated and resented wearing gloves. When quite small I suffered from a thick woollen veil, which was supposed to safeguard the complexion, but my very noisy and

---

[*] Children of both sexes wore sailor suits when small, and boys until they were 11 or 12. Boys were not breeched until much later than at present, and there was at least one occasion when I rejoiced in being taken for my brother by some short-sighted old lady who had the excuse that we were dressed alike and that my hair was at that date cut short like a boy's.

voluble protests soon relieved me of that infliction – old-fashioned and unusual even in those days. I also resented and constantly disobeyed the rule that I must not slide down the banisters or turn head over heels! I had gymnastic lessons, however, and learned to swim, but I yearned for more of the team games which girls did not yet play and suffered a good deal from insufficient outlets for my physical exuberance. Walks in Kensington Gardens and Hyde Park were no adequate substitute, even when enlivened by forbidden tree climbing and jumping of railings, or by games of hide-and-seek.

My father wished me to be educated at home by a governess but luckily yielded to my desire to go to school. When I was just five, I was sent to a neighbouring kindergarten which was kept by a natural history enthusiast, to whose wise guidance my childhood owed an incalculable debt. 'Brownie' as we called her, became a family friend: she spent many holidays with us and even succeeded in persuading my nurse that muddied clothes didn't matter if they were the results of dredging expeditions. From her, I learned to collect everything that crept and crawled: I kept silkworms, spiders (until they got loose in the drawing room), tadpoles and newts; I pressed and named flowers; looked for fossils, collected shells and joined a 'Practical Naturalists' Society'. And when my 'museum' – a glass case with sliding trays and bookshelves on the top of the cabinet – was supplemented by a real microscope, my satisfaction was complete. I learned to make slides, and thereby hangs a truly Victorian tale.

When I was eleven, I discovered a little boy about a year older who had similar tastes. I used to go to tea with him, and to his nurse's horror we spent hours together in his bedroom making slides and looking at them. These highly improper proceedings had to be sanctioned by the parents of both sinners before we could be allowed to seclude ourselves in so unseemly a fashion! Then there were the long and happy hours spent at the Natural History Museum, identifying various specimens and the never-to-be-forgotten afternoon when the Director (he called me 'madam'!) invited me, subject to my nurse's permission, to come downstairs and help his young men to name their shells. I had tea with them and was fully convinced that they needed my assistance, and my brother was not asked too, and altogether it was a delightful and wonderful experience and one which filled me with self-importance.

Kindergarten days over, I was sent to a select private school because Notting Hill High School was at least twenty-five minutes' walk from our home and the nursemaid could not be spared to take and fetch me. Besides I might have made friends there with tradesmen's daughters or someone equally undesirable! However the Doreck College was very good in its old-fashioned way, and I was well taught and spent four happy years there before I was sent, when just fourteen, to Hanover to learn German, and also to be turned into a 'young lady' and acquire some of the feminine accomplishments I refused to have anything to do with at home.

It was not uncommon at that period for girls to be sent abroad to a finishing school, though more often to Paris than elsewhere. The Hanover school to which I went was kept by an English woman, a friend of my mother in their youth, and many girls in our circle went there. It was very cosmopolitan in its clientèle and most of the pupils were between sixteen and eighteen years of age, so I was among the youngest. The teaching and methods were entirely German, and the English head died and was succeeded by a German while I was there. We were thoroughly instructed in modern languages, in German, French and English literature, universal history (not then a subject often taught in English schools) and history of art. Arithmetic was rudimentary, and at fourteen I already knew a good deal more of that subject than my foreign schoolfellows and did not add to my knowledge while there. We learned no Latin and no mathematics or science, but at that date that would probably also have been the case at a private school at home.

What most perturbed me was the unblushing way in which all, except the English girls, read their lessons from books concealed under the desk and otherwise cheated – doubtless because no-one was believed to be truthful without proof. I was of course used to the opposite method: at home every child was trusted unless discovered to be a liar, and I suffered a good deal from the unwonted treatment and its effects on the girls' morale. I also disliked and never got used to the system of favouritism and spying which prevailed, nor to the encouragement of tell-tales. On the whole, however, I was very happy in Hanover and stayed an extra session by my own desire – a fact which made my last year one of continuous spoiling by the authorities, with repeated visits to the theatre and the like, from which my alleged ill-conduct had almost wholly debarred me during my first years at the school. The Hoftheater in Hanover had very good companies, and the performances of classics and modern drama were a pleasant way of improving our knowledge of the language. Twice during the summer holidays I went with the school to the Harz Mountains and on other occasions visited the homes of fellow pupils in other towns.

Kaiser Wilhelm had only recently succeeded to the throne when I went to Hanover, and I well remember how the 'Reise Kaiser' was criticised by his subjects as compared with his father, the 'Weise Kaiser', and his grandfather, the 'Greise Kaiser'.[1] He arrived unexpectedly at Hanover one morning at about 3am and made a tremendous to-do because at that hour there was not a proper turnout of the guard at the barracks. Later in the day, he rode past our *Pensionat* and, to our great satisfaction, stopped to salute our Union Jack. A subsequent memory is of a visit to a former schoolfellow in Berlin who feared I should be arrested for *lèse-majesté* if I expressed my views so openly as I was doing in a café, where they might be overheard.

Apart from school altogether, I had the inestimable benefit of living at home in a house that was full of books, to any and all of which I had access. My mother was herself an omnivorous reader and an exceptionally intelligent woman. Luckily she also held the opinion that it would do far more harm than good to try to control my reading. So I read everything I could lay my hands on – boys' books by Henty, Ballantyne, Kingston, Anthony Hope, Manville Fenn,[2] etc., girls' books (usually very inferior to those meant for boys), nursery classics, such as Miss Edgeworth, Harriet

---

1   1888 was the year of the three Kaisers: Wilhelm I, der greise Kaiser – the old Kaiser; Frederick III, der weise Kaiser – the wise Kaiser; and Wilhelm II, der Reise-Kaiser – the travelling Kaiser (sometimes referred to as 'der Scheisse-Kaiser').

2   Henty, Kingston and Fenn were prolific, writing over 400 novels between them. Ballantyne, best known for *The Coral Island* (1857), had worked for the Hudson's Bay Company and set many of his novels in Canada. Anthony Hope was also prolific but is best remembered for *The Prisoner of Zenda* (1894) and *Rupert of Hentzau* (1898), neither specifically for children.

Martineau, Charlotte Yonge, Mrs Molesworth, Mrs Ewing,[3] and Lewis Carroll; grown-up classics such as Scott, Dickens, George Eliot and Charlotte Brontë; dozens of three-volume trash from Mudie's[4] which had the beneficent result of putting me permanently off that kind of thing later on. I also devoured many books that dated from my mother's childhood or were at any rate old-fashioned in my time – Miss Porter's *Days of Bruce*, *Queechy* and *The Wide Wide World* (many grammar lessons were enlivened by surreptitious counting of the number of times the heroines cried and fainted); Peter Parley's Voyages, Mrs Markham's Histories, even Magnall's Questions, *Little Mary's Grammar* and *The*

3   Maria Edgeworth was a prolific Anglo-Irish novelist and educationist who, with her father, wrote largely moralising stories for early readers. She is best known for *The Parent's Assistant* (1796), a collection of children's stories; and for an adult novel, *Castle Rackrent* (1800). Harriet Martineau was a writer and journalist of radical political and dissenting views, an abolitionist and early sociologist. Her collection of children's stories, *The Playfellow*, was published in 1841. Charlotte Mary Yonge was a prolific and highly regarded English novelist, mainly writing for young girls. Her most popular novel was *The Heir of Redclyffe* (1853), and she edited the girls' magazine *The Monthly Packet* 1851–90. Mrs (Mary Louisa) Molesworth's books were typical of late nineteenth-century writing for girls; her best-known titles are *The Cuckoo Clock* (1877) and *The Carved Lions* (1895). Juliana Horatia Ewing wrote children's stories and several novels, including the bestselling *Jackanapes* (1879), and edited *The Monthly Packet* and *Aunt Judy's Magazine*.

4   Mudie's was a circulating library started in 1842 by Charles Edward Mudie. He became hugely successful by undercutting his rivals, charging at the start only a guinea a year. The library had an enormous hall like the British Museum Reading Room and was comparable in size with a major academic library. It closed in 1937.

Parent's Assistant.[5]

We took in *Little Folks* and the *Boys' Own Paper*; the grown-ups read all the better periodicals from which I was at liberty to extract what I could; my eldest brother was at the period engrossed by Carlyle, RUSKIN and by such lesser reformers as Bellamy and his *Looking Backward*.[6] If I did not read through all of these, at least I knew what they looked like and the kind of thing I could find there. Hugh Miller[7] and Charles Darwin I did tackle seriously, and the first book I ever bought with my own pocket-money, supplemented by a final 2/– from my father, was a complete Shakespeare in thirteen small volumes in a red case. I have it still, much thumbed and rather decrepit but very precious.

5   Jane Porter was the author of *The Scottish Chiefs: A romance* (1811). *Days of Bruce* (1852) was in fact written by Grace Aguilar, an English novelist, poet and writer on Jewish history and religion. *Queechy* (1852) was a sentimental novel by American novelist Elizabeth Wetherell, the pseudonym of Susan Bogert Warner, who also wrote the hugely popular *The Wide Wide World* (1850). American author Samuel Griswold Goodrich's *Peter Parley's Annuals*, which covered geography, history and science, among other subjects, appeared from 1827. Richmal Mangnall's *Historical and Miscellaneous Questions for the Use of Young People* (1800) was generally known as 'Magnall's Questions'. Jane Marcet published many 'Conversations' on mainly scientific subjects, as well as *Mary's Grammar; interspersed with stories, and intended for the use of children* (1835). Mrs Markham was the pseudonym of Elizabeth Penrose, whose history book for children on England (1823/1826) was the most popular textbook of English history for four decades.

6   The American author Edward Bellamy's utopian science fiction novel *Looking Backward: 2000–1887* (1888) was a bestseller in its time and has remained in print ever since. It became hugely influential shortly after publication, prompting the emergence of a political movement; it also inspired a number of utopian communities.

7   The geologist, writer, folklorist and evangelical Christian Hugh Miller wrote several geological works and disagreed with Darwinian evolutionary theory, expressing in his book *Footprints of the Creator* (1849) his view that the different species were not the result of evolution but the work of a benevolent creator.

We 'did' Shakespeare plays at school in the old Clarendon Press edition, and to this day I know most of *Henry V* by heart – the first complete play I studied. Not even analysis and parsing of the great speeches and learning all the abstruse 'notes' verbatim could spoil the thrill of the poetry. How well I remember teaching Nurse the speeches by heart while she brushed my hair in the mornings, and how I loved to declaim 'Friends, Romans, Countrymen' to anyone who would listen, or for my own delectation when no-one could be found. My father was very strict about slang and bad language. But what could be said to my shout of 'The devil damn thee black, thou cream-faced loon'. 'That's Shakespeare?'

Except needlework, French, music and dancing, I loved all my lessons, even learning the queens of England, or jingles about battles of the Wars of the Roses, or the capitals and rivers of the countries of Europe or of the British counties, but Shakespeare came far away first. Once in the Christmas holidays some brothers and cousins and I went to the house of Miss Cowen, the actress (and a family friend) and read and acted with her *A Midsummer Night's Dream*. What fun it was to be Hermia and abuse the hapless Helena! Those were the days of Irving and Ellen Terry, and we were taken to see them act at least once a year, and whatever the ornateness of the staging or the unwarranted alterations of the text, nothing could spoil the plays in a child's eyes. Irving as Richard III or Shylock, Ellen Terry in any and every part she adorned – these were revelations which nothing can efface or render less memorable.

Of course our 'treats' were not always of so improving a nature. The zoo (with a ride on the elephant or camel), fireworks at the Crystal Palace, German Reeds with Corney

Grain and Grossmith, Maskelyne and Cooke's[8], Mme Tussaud's, Gilbert and Sullivan (*The Mikado* when it first appeared was my first play, in the evening of such a snowy day that it was doubtful if my grandmother's coachman could get us to the theatre), pantomimes at the Aquarium (Drury Lane pantomimes were considered too vulgar for us children), circuses, magic lantern shows at the Polytechnic[9] – we sampled and enjoyed them all, even a stage adaptation of the sentimental *Little Lord Fauntleroy*. Nor must the Lord Mayor's Show days be forgotten, when a relative invited all his young friends to view the procession from his warehouse in the City, entertaining them afterwards to a sumptuous spread.

Once every summer Grannie took us to Buszard's[10] for strawberries and cream and ices – an event not to be under-estimated by those who have been used to tea-shops and

8   Thomas German Reed founded his German Reed Entertainments company in 1855, providing gentle, intelligent, comic musical entertainment suitable for children. Corney Grain was a member of the German Reeds and a singer and performer of comic musical sketches at the piano. George Grossmith was a great friend and rival of his, and the original singer of most of the patter songs in Gilbert and Sullivan, despite having no singing voice. He was also joint author with his brother of *The Diary of a Nobody* (1892). John Nevil Maskelyne and George Alfred Cooke were English magicians who invented many illusions still performed today. They made their theatrical debut in 1865. Maskelyne was also a successful inventor; among many others, he took out a patent on a coin-operated lock for public lavatories (1892), which was used in England until the 1950s.

9   The Royal Polytechnic Institution was famous for its spectacular magic lantern shows. It had huge screens and provided accompanying musicians and a team of people to produce sound effects to enhance the performance.

10 Buszard's cake shop was located at the west end of Oxford Street. They became famous for setting up tables and chairs in Hyde Park during the 1851 exhibition, serving drinks and cakes.

restaurant meals all their lives. In my young days there was nowhere where one could drop in to lunch or tea as a matter of course and ordinary middle-class folk went home or to their friends for tea, unless on some very special occasion. I remember many, many years later, on the day when the then Duke of York (George V) married Princess May (Queen Mary), one of my brothers and I stood for hours in the crowd to see them drive to and from Westminster Abbey. On our way home, tired and thirsty, we walked all down Regent Street and Oxford Street before we were able at last to get a cup of tea at the corner of North Audley Street close to Marble Arch. There had literally been nowhere else to go.

Another frequent summer expedition was a drive to Richmond with my grandmother; this included always a visit to the Maid of Honour cake shop, a stroll in the Park to see the deer and sometimes an hour in a boat on the river. Every year too we went to Kew Gardens and sometimes for Sunday afternoon walks in the country with Brownie or my father. When the Metropolitan Railway was extended to Rickmansworth, then a village, I remember a visit there because for the first time I saw a man in a smock-frock who pulled his forelock as a mark of respect to the gentry. Another country jaunt stands out in my memory because of a fight with the big brother who was taking me and who, in spite of the heat and the smelly inside, would not allow me to go on the top of the bus because of the impropriety for a girl of such a proceeding. I had to submit as the only alternative to an ignominious return home.

In one matter, however, we were allowed to ignore convention; I suppose we were almost the first 'respectable' children to take out picnic teas in the Gardens on warm summer afternoons. Very often we dashed off afterwards to meet our father on his way home and to dive into the tail pockets of his frock coat to see if he had brought us a box of Lombard chocolates. 'Wait a minute, wait a minute, until I hear whether you have been good children'. But we never had, so we seized on the delectable oblong pieces of chocolate in their paper wrappings with a blue bee on the outside before there was time for adverse reports. The frock coat and high hat were my father's invariable costume in London: never, until he retired at the age of seventy, did I see him otherwise clad in Town, and even in the country he never wore 'knickerbockers'. He celebrated his retirement by the purchase of a square bowler,[11] much to the distress of my mother and self, who regarded it as an outrage. It was only after his retirement that he would be seen carrying even the smallest parcel, that being incompatible with professional dignity. Similarly with smoking – and he was an inveterate smoker. He lit his pipe as he entered the Park on his way to the West End, and he carefully extinguished it when he reached Grosvenor Gate. When he got to his consulting rooms, he changed his coat and ate a pastille so that no odour of smoke should hang about him. Nor did he smoke again until in the Park on his way home. The embargo on a cigar would not have been so severe, but 'gentlemen' could not publicly indulge in pipe smoking, and cigars were not only an extravagance but also much less satisfying.

My father was an ardent Conservative to whom the name and thought of Gladstone were anathema and Home Rule an inconceivable outrage. My earliest political recollection is of the death of Beaconsfield.[12] My father was tossing me in his arms and I, rather giddy, was nearing the ceiling when I heard him say to Nurse, 'Well, Barker, what do you think

11 Square bowlers were worn by coachmen, hence the outrage.

12 Benjamin Disraeli (1st Lord Beaconsfield), statesman and novelist, was Prime Minister briefly in 1868 and 1874–80. William Ewart Gladstone was a Liberal statesman and four times Prime Minister (1868–74, 1880–85, 1886 and 1892–4).

about the death of Dizzy?' I suppose I thought there was some reference to my sensations at the moment – anyway I have never forgotten the event, though I do not remember the Fenian outrages nor the murder of the Czar[13] which took place within the year. Another unforgotten date is that of the battle of Tel el-Kebir.[14] The one thing I really feared was men shouting out news after I was in bed, and that was what happened on that Sunday, Barker's Sunday out, and to add to my grievance, it was on my birthday – the ninth – when nothing ought to have been allowed to frighten me and make me unhappy. Yet another remembered political happening is being taken by my father to hear a speech by Lord Randolph Churchill.[15] I have no idea of the subject and no recollection of the speaker, but I know the meeting was after dark – I suppose on a winter afternoon – and at Paddington Baths[16], and that I went alone with my father and sat on his shoulder so that I might see.

13 Czar Alexander II was assassinated March 1881; the Fenian bombing campaign was from 1881 to 1885.

14 The battle of Tel el-Kebir (or Tell al-Qabir) was part of the war fought between Britain and Egypt in 1882. The nationalist movement under Urabi strongly resented British and French interference in Egypt's affairs, while the British were anxious to keep and protect the Suez Canal. It occurred on 13th September 1882 (not the 9th, as Morley seems to have thought).

15 Lord Randolph Henry Spencer-Churchill was a British statesman and father of Winston Churchill.

16 Paddington public baths and washhouses were situated at Queen's Road Bayswater, close to the Queen's Road [now Queensway] and Royal Oak Stations. 'There is ... a 1st class swimming-bath for ladies, and private baths the same as for men. There is also a private laundry, where persons may have the use of tubs, hot and cold water, steam-wringers, drying chambers, irons, and mangles, at a charge of 1 ½ d. per hour.' In addition the building rented a hall for meetings.

I was nearly twelve at the time of Queen Victoria's Jubilee, but the news of an uncle's death arrived while I was helping to decorate the balcony with flags and fairy lamps, so we did not go to see the procession next day. It still amuses me to remember that this disappointment did not prevent me writing the best composition on the subject, though I was the only girl in my class who had not seen it.

The Queen seems to play a great part in my childish recollections. It was my grandmother's frequent habit to drive with me up and down the Park until the Queen had gone by, and we children sometimes went to Paddington Station when there was a royal migration to Windsor. Queen Victoria may have passed through a period of unpopularity in earlier times, but that was long before, and all through my childhood and until she died, she stood, for most of her subjects, as the visible symbol for their love and loyalty to the Empire to which they were proud to belong. In the eighties and nineties we had no doubts of its justification and greatness, and the Queen was its protagonist and the beloved mother of its peoples. Her death in 1901 was rightly felt to mark the end of an epoch, but it was also mourned as a personal loss by almost all her subjects. The day of her funeral procession was one of profound gloom; Londoners wore only black, and I have always thought Mr Noel Coward's whistling errand-boy episode in *Cavalcade* untrue to fact. I do not think any London boy, however light-hearted or thoughtless, would have whistled on that day.

I saw the procession from a stand in Hamilton Gardens and well remember that though the Park was black with spectators as far as the eye could reach, and even in the trees, there was such absolute quiet that one could hear the tramp of the soldiers' feet as they marched down Piccadilly and turned in at Hyde Park Corner on their way through Marble Arch to Paddington Station. When the procession passed us, the Kaiser was doing his best to draw level with the King, who, as chief mourner, naturally was intended to ride immediately behind the gun carriage on which the coffin was borne. I believe that little bid for precedence went on throughout the slow march, but King Edward held his own with unobtrusive and dignified determination.

CHAPTER 2:

Home life

We lived, as I have said, in Bayswater, in Craven Hill Gardens, where the family had settled several years before my birth. The house was my grandmother's, and my father was her tenant. As the family thus consisted of three adults and six young folk of very varying ages (there were twenty-five years between eldest and youngest), we necessarily required a large house. Ours contained nine bedrooms and a dressing room, six sitting rooms, including the nursery, and a large basement with kitchen, pantry and servants' sitting room. There was one fixed bath on the same floor as my parents' bedroom, and all water had to be carried to the two floors above. My mother had never previously lived in a house with a fixed bath so this did not appear to her as a hardship, and I do not remember that there were ever complaints on this score until well on into the present century. In my young days, the servants did not use the bathroom, and their own room was two flights of stairs above. So were the night nursery and three of our bedrooms, and in retrospect the amount of water-carrying and slop-emptying fills me with horror. Then it all seemed taken for granted by everyone concerned – even the three daily hip-baths which were used by my grandmother and eldest brother.

Similarly every bit of food had to be carried up seventeen stone stairs from kitchen to dining room, and tea things one-and-a-half flights higher still to the drawing room. Nursery dinners were taken up eighty-odd stairs; though as there was a small range in the nursery, other meals were prepared there. The servants were saved some running up and down stairs by a 'whistle' and speaking-tube from hall to nursery.*

From basement to the top of the house (there were no attics) there were 105 stairs, and 65 from hall to nursery. It was also in other respects very inconvenient, with a long stone passage and a yard back and front in the basement; a long tiled hall running the whole width of the house, and wide landings on every floor except the two top ones. This meant much waste of space and extra labour. In addition, the rooms were badly planned, and the rest of the house was sacrificed to the drawing room, an immense double room, divided by curtains, the whole of which was never used except for large parties – scarcely a dozen times in our occupation of over half a century. My coming-out dance of some 250 people was comfortably accommodated in it. On normal occasions the front drawing room, with its three enormous sash windows from ceiling to floor, was big enough for all requirements, and, in fact, even that was used only at weekends, partly because of the difficulty of warming it adequately with its one open grate. (There was a second grate in the back drawing room.) However the balcony was a great asset on warm evenings, for we had not even the tiniest of gardens. We faced the square, but unfortunately also the backs of the houses built in it after ours had been purchased. Though we of course had the right of entry to the square, much used by us young ones in the summer, our view of it was completely blocked. And there was no sun in any of our rooms except

---

* We had the telephone installed earlier than most of our friends, about 1903 or 1904, because, as my father was fond of explaining to visitors, it was essential that my doctor brother could be called up if needed when he was dining with us. Wireless, of course, did not exist until much later and I sometimes wonder how we managed to endure the First World War without it. I well remember that the first time I listened in was at a Reading neighbour's house in 1926 during the General Strike of that year, when no newspapers were published.

the drawing room, nursery – much the nicest room in the house – and my parents' bedroom. The dining room was also a good size and eighteen people could be comfortably served at table on occasions – which occurred very seldom. The other two sitting rooms on the ground floor, the smoking room and morning room, were dark and small, with engraved glass windows to shut out the yard wall and the houses close behind in the next street. The other sitting room, the boudoir, was a converted conservatory, small and overcrowded with furniture, but the room habitually used in the evenings by the elders, and by us until we grew up and betook ourselves to greater comfort elsewhere.

Upstairs, there were two over-large and two poky bedrooms on each floor. My own, when I was grown up, which had once served as night nursery for Nurse and two or three children, made a very good bed-sitting-room, with a sofa, three bookcases, two big cupboards, a full-size wardrobe, table and roll-top desk as well as all bedroom furniture. But two of my brothers had tiny slips which had obviously been designed as dressing rooms and were quite unfit to house grown men. The two younger ones shared a very large front room on the top floor. The back room on that floor, also very large, accommodated three servants, and when we grew older and slept alone, the old nurse had a dressing room to herself on the same floor. Ultimately the cook also had a similar room.

Until after my grandmother's death in 1912, the house was lit by gas, which my father turned off at the main at 11pm. When I was very young, there were only the old burners with their sizzling blue flames. Later, these were replaced by Sugg's burners[17] and, later still, by incandescent

---

17 William Sugg & Co, founded in 1837, were pioneers in the development of gas lighting using the Argand burner principle.

lights with by-passes. And some time in my remote youth, before I remember, an old-fashioned gas-fire was installed in the smoking room. Everywhere else there were open grates, so that coal had to be carried all over the house, as well as water. But the coachman did that, not the maid-servants. At some stage, long after I was grown-up, gas fires were put in three of the bedrooms, but my mother and grandmother used them only under compulsion, and I mine practically not at all, although I worked in my room.

In the dining room we used a colza-lamp chandelier[18], and when there were visitors, candles all round it in addition: in the boudoir and drawing room there were also lamps, as my mother did not like gas. Needless to say, filling and trimming the lamps occasioned much additional labour.

Cooking and bath water heating were both accomplished by means of a large, old-fashioned kitchen range. Since the fire was extinguished carefully before the servants went to bed at ten o'clock, the water was often not adequately heated for my father's morning bath, when he was no longer allowed the cold plunge which he enjoyed until middle age. (We young ones, like other Victorian children, all took daily cold baths winter and summer). As I look back, the recurring grumble about insufficiently heated bath water is my chief recollection of domestic difficulty. Nowadays we should consider that we were understaffed, and that the servants were underpaid and shockingly overworked. But apparently they did not think so, according to the prevailing standards. They stayed with us for many, many years, and when they left, usually to be married, they remained friends who came back to visit us.

18 Colza lamps were oil burning, using a vegetable oil produced from rape seeds.

Thus my nurse came when I was five and stayed till she died at the age of eighty-seven in 1916; my grandmother's useful maid was with her for some fifteen years or more; I remember one cook named Gray (she used to make us bread mice with currant eyes) who seems to dominate the kitchen of my childish memories, and to whose seaside home after she had left us we went to recuperate after measles or chicken-pox. And there was a housemaid named Mary who was with us for years, and the coachman who came when, at seventy, my grandmother started a one-horse hired carriage, and stayed until she died a quarter of a century later. Even the charwoman, Mrs Bailey, was a faithful servitor, and ultimately her daughter, Georgina, came to us as nursery-maid – her first place – at the princely remuneration of £6 a year. My mother was very upset when a servant had to be replaced, but there were always several applications for the vacancy, and it was possible to insist on one's requirements, and to make one's choice; it was the invariable practice to have a personal interview with the former employer regarding character. Moreover notice was given as a matter of course for disobedience to orders or for bad work. Thus we lost one excellent parlour-maid because she went behind the disinfection curtain to visit a scarlet-fever patient.

That incident recalls the fact that not only were all childish ailments dealt with at home, but that Barker would have violently resented the introduction of a hospital nurse. By day and by night and for seven days a week, she cared for her sick children, and she would infallibly have left on the spot had it been suggested she was unable to do so, either through lack of skill or because the strain was too great without additional help. Every family of our acquaintance possessed a nanny, the autocrat of the nursery, the children's 'second mother' often equally beloved and, in early years, much more omnipresent and apparently omnipotent than the mother herself. But I still believe that we were peculiarly fortunate in ours. Ignorant in book-learning, able to write and to spell, but not do both together because, so she said, she was taught in her youth to do only one thing at a time, Barker possessed nevertheless a fund of common-sense and of psychological insight into child-nature which, combined with her never-failing love and sympathy and absolute loyalty to her trust, rendered her an ideal guide, philosopher and friend to little children.

This is not the place in which to attempt to draw her portrait at full length. But I want to make it clear that in the ordinary professional middle-class household the Victorian mistress was not occupied with the detailed personal care of her children. She superintended, of course, but it would have been unheard of for her to bath her baby, to push out the pram, even to play with the children except at stated hours. We went for walks with both our parents much more frequently than did most of our acquaintances with theirs; my mother came up to the nursery every morning and we went downstairs for an hour or so after tea. When we were old enough to eat properly, we had our dinner in the dining room at lunch time; later on we went down to dessert in the evening. But most of our early lives were spent in the nursery under the immediate authority of the nurse, and that was the case with all the children of families similarly circumstanced.

Nor, however excellent a housewife, was the mistress of such a house as ours expected or permitted by the cook to spend much time in the kitchen. My own mother was a most competent housekeeper, a first-rate manager and expert needlewoman. She went into the basement every morning, put away and gave out the stores herself,[*] examined the state

---

[*]   These were locked up, and tea, sugar, etc. measured out and distributed daily.

of the larder, gave orders to the cook and wrote down the daily menus. But those duties accomplished and the linen put away or taken out, she did not, if she could avoid it, risk incurring the cook's resentment by going down the kitchen stairs again that day. If the necessity arose, she called down or rang for the cook to come up if a message would not suffice.

My mother spent a great deal of her time in mending, darning and patching indefatigably; she could not cut out or make clothes but she knitted all the socks for her husband and four sons who never, except in evening dress, wore any she had not made; she did the household shopping and went all over London in order to place her orders most profitably. During spring-cleaning she washed her best glass and china as well as the drawing room ornaments, and she dusted all the numerous books until I was old enough to assist her. She also attended to the few plants and arranged the meagre supply of flowers. But in the ordinary way, neither she nor any other woman in her position either cooked or cleaned or 'minded' her children. Not until I was in my thirties had I ever seen a London mother of our own class push her baby's perambulator in the streets, and I still remember the shock of surprise I underwent when, for the first time in my experience, a friend opened her own front door when I went to call. I was not allowed to do so even if I happened to be in the hall when the bell rang and knew who was likely to be there.

In a large mixed household like ours, where there was no money to spare, the mistress was fully occupied if, like my mother, she was so inclined and also had full responsibility for the children's upbringing and education. But there were very many mistresses of Victorian households who had not enough to do, and who had no sensible employment for their many leisure hours. This was particularly the case where there was no lack of means and therefore no need for planning and economising. Hence the dull ritual of 'calling' on at-home days and the carefully regulated interchange of visits between people who had no desire to see one another except as a means of killing time.

Whatever may or may not be its justification, the outcry against married women continuing their professional careers lest their household and children be neglected cannot be raised by those who are aware of actual conditions fifty or sixty years ago. Efficient nannies and large families being equal rarities nowadays, public nurseries are the obvious present-day alternatives; similarly, domestic conditions having changed in other respects, cheap labour being – happily – unobtainable, private kitchens uneconomical, and home manufacture, whether of food or clothes, for the most part superseded, it is necessary and desirable to find other sources of supply.

Comparison with past conditions does not prove that either the homes or those who run them will necessarily suffer by a subdivision of labour and specialisation of function which should enable every wife and mother to follow the career, whether domestic or professional, for which she is best adapted. One type of work is as worthy as another, but not every individual is equally competent to perform all. This applies to both men and women, married or single, and marriage and motherhood as such should not be regarded as careers but the fulfilment of human and physical needs. The best work, domestic or any other, is best performed by those who choose it as their means of earning a livelihood and are adequately trained to undertake it. This was long ago recognised with regard to teaching and sick-nursing: it is gradually obtaining recognition for nursery nurses and cooks, and it is equally true for every other type of domestic worker. It is also obvious that an artist or a medical woman, a teacher or a lawyer, a sanitary inspector or a psychiatrist who is interested in her job will not become an efficient house-keeper merely because she has been forced to relinquish her chosen work as a result of marriage and motherhood.

CHAPTER 3

External conditions

It will already have become apparent that the London of my childhood differed materially from the London of today. For one thing, there was a much more definite cleavage between the various social classes, and strict lines were drawn between the people one did or did not 'know'. Thus professional men did not mix with those in retail trade, nor were they and their families commonly received in equal terms by those in 'Society'. The upper middle class did not mingle with the lower, and neither 'visited' the 'poor', a phrase which lumped together superior artisans and skilled workers with unskilled labourers and the 'submerged tenth'. In the country, the barriers between 'county' families and the rest were even more insuperable, and the feudal conditions regulating the relations between landlords and tenants of every degree lingered on to an extent almost incredible to the present generation. The divisions which still survive, only faintly suggest those which obtained well into the present century.

A 'gentleman' or a 'lady' – and the words were still in common use and bore a definite significance – accepted certain conventions of behaviour, dress and outlook as part of the natural order, and one no more thought of contravening them than of putting a knife in the mouth or calling a 'napkin' a 'serviette,' or a 'servant' a 'maid'. It had to be a very bold young man to appear in the streets without a hat; a girl who went out, even in summer, without gloves exposed herself to biting criticism. I well remember when I was at college being exhorted to attend carefully to such details of dress, lest I made it more difficult for other girls to obtain permission to study, and therefore to become 'queer' and unlike other people.

Drunkenness was a common vice among women as well as men, and the newly established Bank Holidays[19] were days to be dreaded on this account by respectable people. As children, we were not allowed in the gardens or parks on such occasions because of what we might encounter; and my sister-in-law tells me she was brought up in the belief that 'ladies' stopped at home on Bank Holidays. Beggars, too, were at all times to be seen in the streets, and included the very old and the very young, babies being often hired out to adults as a means of eliciting alms. There were also numerous crossing-sweepers and street bootblacks, and very necessary they were in those days of filthy and muddy streets.

London mud and the town smell of horse dung are pungent memories of my youth. How well I recall the horrible stench that assailed one's nostrils as one came up the slope from Paddington Station on a summer evening! The smell of petrol is pleasant in comparison, and whatever the dangers and drawbacks of motor-cars in crowded cities, the present-day street cleanliness of London is certainly attributable to their introduction. For mud disappeared with the coming of tarred roads, just as the dust-whitened hedgerows of the country gave way to their natural green. Early women bicyclists either wrapped their heads in scarves or faced the necessity of a shampoo after a country spin, while skids owing to the mud were daily experiences in both town and country.

Fogs were another source and result of London dirt, and a fog in the eighties and nineties was of the pea-soup variety, opaque, yellow, something to be smelled and tasted, and quite impenetrable by the human eye. Boys with flares

19   Bank holidays were first instituted in 1871.

guided foot-passengers, who often completely lost their bearings. I remember, for example, that my father on one such occasion inadvertently walked into the Round Pond, which was quite out of the route he thought he was taking. We children rejoiced in a fog because our nurse sent us to school with a huge Buzzard peppermint – the sort that were sold four-a-penny – in our mouths and a comforter tied round them to prevent conversation. Modern modes of heating have abolished the worst variety of London fog, much to the advantage of health and cleanliness.

Getting about London, especially on Sundays, entailed much more difficulty and planning than today in order to avoid long waits between 'bus and Underground. The Metropolitan Railway was of course already there in my childhood, but I well remember its extension north-west from Baker Street and the opening of the Hampstead stations and those at Northwood, Pinner and Rickmansworth – all of them still country villages. The 'buses of my youth were many-coloured and added considerably to the gay appearance of the streets. The old knife-board variety,[20] scaled by a sort of ladder, with the passengers seated in two rows, back to back, on the outside, and with dirty straw on the floor inside, were replaced in my early days by a more modern construction with a staircase that could be mounted in seemly fashion by women as well as men.

I still regret the old uncovered outside seats, which provided an unmatched view of the streets and on which I have taken many a pleasant ride in former days. But the inside of the horse-drawn bus, with its jerks and smells, was another matter, and no-one can question the superior attraction of the motor variety, even when most crowded and full of

20 A type of horse-drawn omnibus with upper deck back-to-back seating. Seating on the roofs of buses began around 1845, and the knifeboard variety was in use by 1862.

strap-hangers. Modern drivers and conductors are not such racy companions as their predecessors, whose picturesque language and power of repartee added so much to the life of the town and made them the rightful heirs of Sam Weller[21] and his traditions.

Few probably could find it in their hearts to regret the old growler,[22] with its frequently broken springs, its dirty straw and cushions, rattling windows and often crusty coachman. But the hansom cab was in another category altogether, and I know nothing today to exceed the thrill of the drive before its opened glass, the trotting horse and the smart perched-up cabby behind with whom one communicated through an intriguing trap-door in the roof. Whatever danger there may have been in this mode of progression – and I do not remember to have heard of many accidents – was more than balanced by the excitement and sense of adventure one felt as the horse threaded his way through the traffic and over-took his rivals. The clop-clop of his hoofs on the macadam-ised roads, or on the wooden blocks which replaced them in crowded thoroughfares, is still a treasured memory. When, *ca.* 1910, taxicabs first plied for hire, our street – which was a cul-de-sac – proved a popular place for turning. We used to flock to the front windows to watch the performance. Similarly, in August 1914, just after the declaration of war, when a plane circled over the hotel at Hindhead where I happened to be staying, everyone got up from lunch for the first sight of the novel phenomenon.

21   A Cockney character in Dickens' first novel, *The Pickwick Papers* (1837).

22   The growler was officially called the Clarence, its nickname deriving (possibly) from the noise it made over cobbles. It was an enclosed, glass-fronted, four-wheeled carriage, drawn by two horses and seating four passengers, with plenty of room for luggage. It was used as a vehicle for hire, with a coachman.

Another memory – different in kind – is of the Annual Meet of the Four-in-Hand Club,[23] when coaches assembled just inside the Park between Victoria Gate and Marble Arch before they set off on their race to Brighton, or wherever it was. My recollection concerns only the meet, when one could imagine oneself back in the times of Pickwick or Tom Brown[24] and taste vicariously the joys of the rush over open roads. There usually hovered in the neighbourhood on these occasions a bright yellow family barouche of the type most fashionable forty or fifty years earlier. I have no idea to whom it belonged, but afternoon frequenters of the parks in my childhood were well acquainted with its unusual shape and colour. The coachman and footman still wore big powdered wigs, so that for a small girl the whole turn-out recalled the joys of the Lord Mayor's Show.

The tandems and dogcarts driven by fashionable young men, often wearing white high hats, were another source of amusement, especially when there was a diminutive, many-buttoned little 'tiger'[25] at the back of the vehicle. Nor must we omit from the picture the old penny-farthing bicycle, with its rider perched on and frequently tumbling off the big front wheel. It was a perennial joy when one hove in sight either in park or street, and I well remember watching from the nursery window my eldest brother's efforts to learn to balance himself on one of them.

23 A driving club founded in 1856 and restricted in membership. It met at least twice during the season 'to drive down to some place for dinner'. Meetings were originally held in Hyde Park, but were later moved to Horse Guards Parade as they were causing an obstruction to traffic.

24 Samuel Pickwick was one of the central characters in Dickens' *The Pickwick Papers*, Tom Brown the hero of Thomas Hughes' *Tom Brown's School Days* (1857).

25 A tiger was a groom in striped livery who rode behind his employer in smaller vehicles in order to hold or walk the horses when they were not being driven. It was a status symbol to have the youngest, smallest tiger.

In some respects London was much noisier than nowadays. Street cries had not entirely disappeared, and lavender-, watercress- and muffin-sellers still frequented the streets at appropriate times of the year, while the milkman's or chimney sweep's announcement of his presence was still loudly vocal. By the way, there were still two mangy cows in Hyde Park whose woman attendant would milk them for intending purchasers. There were, too, many more street musicians than there are today, loud brass 'German bands',[26] countless organ-grinders with monkeys, individuals who played half-a-dozen instruments at once – cymbals, drums, bells and what-not; bagpipe players in Highland costume, etc. etc. There were also much more frequent Punch and Judy shows at street corners, and these might on occasion be paid to perform outside one's own dining room windows; street jugglers were comparatively common; on May Day there were still occasional Jacks-in-the-Green[27] and on 5th November countless Guy Fawkes, while in the summer we were asked to 'remember the grotto'.[28] Even town criers making announcements in old-fashioned livery and with a big bell were not unknown, though I think they were

26 There were two types of German brass bands: some were seasonal, brought over in the summer from Germany, others were groups of German immigrants.

27 Jacks-in-the-green were part of the traditional May Day celebrations, mostly urban and concentrated in London. They were enacted by chimney sweeps, and the most prominent feature was a man inside a wooden or basketwork framework decorated with flowers and greenery so that he resembled a conical bush with feet.

28 Oyster festivals throughout the country marked the beginning of the oyster season in late July and August. In London, 'Oyster Day' – 4th August – was of great importance to Georgian and Victorian Londoners, who rushed to get hold of the first oyster available. Children from the poorer parts of London collected the discarded shells and used them to construct 'grottos', occasionally lit by a candle. Passers-by would then be accosted to 'remember the grotto' by putting a few coins in an empty oyster shell.

commoner in seaside towns and in watering places than in London. Hawkers with toys and puzzles and the like lined most shopping thoroughfares, not only at Christmas as nowadays, and they and the newsboys shouted their wares apparently without restriction. Fire engines, also with bells, dashed wildly through the streets when there was occasion.

Another noise which I recall, no doubt from the days of the Trafalgar Square riots[29] and the big dock strike in the eighties, is the sound of tramping feet and the lugubrious chant of the marchers proclaiming that 'We got no work to do, we got no work to do, we're all hard working men and we got no work to do'. In my young days the social conscience was becoming very much alive to the 'condition of England' question of which these men were an offshoot, and I grew up in a milieu which was deeply stirred by such social portents. My eldest brother was one of the original Associates of Toynbee Hall[30] and a friend of **CANON AND MRS BARNETT** whom he assisted in the formation and running of the first London Boys' Club, in Leman Street, Whitechapel. Later on he was instrumental in starting other boys' clubs in the

29 In 1886 and 1887, Trafalgar Square became a rallying point for protests against economic hardship by the poor and unemployed of London. Organised by the Social Democratic Federation, the protestors were supported by middle class socialists including Annie Besant, G.B. Shaw and William Morris. On 13 November 1887, the police charged the assembled protestors, causing many casualties. The events on this day became known as 'Bloody Sunday'. There was a further protest a week later.

30 Toynbee Hall was created in 1884 by Samuel Barnett, a Church of England curate, and his wife Henrietta, in response to a growing realisation that enduring social change needed a radical vision. Located in Commercial Street, Whitechapel, they created a place for university students and graduates to live and work as volunteers in London's East End, bringing them face to face with poverty, and giving them the opportunity to develop practical solutions that they could take with them into national life. Clement Attlee and William Beveridge were two national leaders who worked at Toynbee Hall.

East End of London, while my second brother founded and was for many years the Hon. Secretary of the biggest boys' club in the West Central district. It was my eldest brother who brought home such books as Bellamy's *Looking Backward*, Booth's *Darkest England* and Ruskin's *Unto this Last*,[31] and it was these, coupled with the example set me by my elders, that first fired my interest in social conditions. With other girls in our circle, I began going to 'Happy Evenings', today known as Play Centres, as soon as I came home from school; later on I collected children's pennies at a neighbouring elementary school as a contribution towards their country holiday; I visited for the ICAA[32] and ran classes at clubs for girls and boys.

These first essays in social work may or may not have been of much benefit to other people. They were of inestimable value to myself in that they inspired me for the first time with interest in social and political matters and gave me my earliest insight into the meaning of citizenship and its duties. At college this interest was strengthened by our gild work at St Helen's Settlement, Stratford-atte-Bowe,[33] and

31 The best-selling *In Darkest England and the Way Out* (1890) by William Booth, founder of the Salvation Army, puts forward the social welfare strategies that formed the basis of the work of the Salvation Army. John Ruskin's *Unto this Last* (1860/1862) proposed the application of moral justice to nineteenth-century economics, bearing in mind the interests of both 'master and labourer'.

32 The Invalid Children's Aid Association was founded in 1888 to provide help for disabled children. It was staffed largely by volunteers, some of whom visited poor homes in the East End to give basic lessons to children who through disability were unable to attend school. It also helped to find convalescent home places for such children. By 1891 it was able to employ staff and over the years extended its range of support. It still exists under the name ICAN.

33 St Helen's House women's settlement was founded in 1896 in The Grove, Stratford, with similar aims to Toynbee Hall.

by our parties arranged for their club-girls at Kensington. I shall not easily forget the impression made on all of us by the fact that these girls, driving westwards in a private omnibus, thought that they were in the country when they first saw the grass and green trees of Hyde Park. That kind of experience aroused doubts and questioning in the minds of young people who were learning to think for themselves. We did not all reach the same conclusions or adopt the same political views, but I think we did all begin to realise for ourselves the meaning of our social privileges and the duty incumbent upon us in one way or another to work for the betterment of those whose lot had been cast in very different surroundings.

The spirit of the times was the spirit of reform, and one could not be young and keen without coming under its influence.

CHAPTER 4:

Education and emancipation

The battle for girls' education had to a large extent been won before my own turn came. The Cambridge and Oxford Colleges for women were firmly established, women were admitted to London degrees and Bedford College had been opened since 1849. **MISS BEALE** and **MISS BUSS** between them had already revolutionised girls' education, and the Girls' Public Day Schools [GPDS][34] were recognised and flourishing institutions. So when I first went to school in 1880 it was the usual thing for sensible parents to require that their girls should be properly taught by educated women, even when a governess at home was preferred to the social 'mixture' found in a school environment. In my own case both my parents were determined that I should have every educational advantage they could procure for me, and, since I was sent to boarding school for three years and my four brothers were all day boys at University College School, my preliminary education was more expensive than theirs.

My father did not profess to know much about academic learning. All my brothers were expected to pass the London matriculation examination as a preliminary to their professional or other training, but lack of means precluded the idea of any of them proceeding to Oxford or Cambridge, which at that date were alone recognised as affording 'university' education – at any rate in the social sense of the term. My father was quite willing for my own school career to terminate

34 The Girls' Public Day School Trust was set up originally as a company in 1872. Its aim was to establish high schools for girls of all classes that provided a high standard of academic, as well as moral and religious education. Already by 1880 it had opened twenty-two schools, half in the London area and half elsewhere.

in the same way as the boys'. After that I do not suppose he had planned anything for me other than a year or two of social life before I married and 'settled down'. My mother's ambitions for me were similar, but since she had pined all her life for an intellectual outlet, she had more understanding of my own views even though she did not approve of them.

Though my mother was born in 1840 and was married in 1860, she had herself enjoyed an unusually good education for a girl of her period. Apart from her honeymoon and one long summer holiday in Switzerland, she very rarely went abroad, except for a few visits to Paris and the week spent in taking me for the first time to Hanover. But she spoke French and German fluently, corresponded regularly with her sister in the latter language until the First World War and read a great many foreign books of all kinds until the end of her life. She was also widely read in English literature and history, and though she had not been allowed to learn Latin as she wished, she had been permitted to study elementary algebra – a fact of which she was inordinately proud. To the end of her days, she preserved a number of exercise books filled with her essays on a great variety of subjects, and there was no doubt that she was much better and much more systematically taught than most young ladies of her day. Consequently she sympathised with my intellectual interests, and though she did not approve of my determination to have an independent career, I always thought she was rather jealous of my success in getting my own way in this respect. For she did not ever enjoy her daily domestic round, and fulfilled her tasks from a sense of duty, not from choice or inclination.

When at the age of seventeen I left school, I was a year too young to 'come out', and the question of occupation at once arose. Having been abroad for three years, I had no English girlfriends, and even my brothers, two already at work and one fully employed at school, were not available for constant companionship. There was little or nothing for me to do in the house as I still detested sewing; I was not allowed to go out alone, even across the road to post a letter, and whatever my mother would have preferred, she had long been accustomed to drive with my grandmother for two-and-a-half hours each afternoon – a habit which could not easily be broken.* I not only hated the mental and physical stagnation of these daily drives but, by great good luck, as it turned out for my future, was always sick if I occupied the back seat of the carriage for any length of time.

---

* 'Grannie' was a most important figure in our home-life, much beloved by all her grandchildren and the fount and source of many childish treats. She lived with us from the time she became a widow, several years before my birth. Then only in her fifties, she was henceforward regarded as an old lady. I never saw her without the cap which in her youth was the household sign of married status, as was the bonnet out of doors. She was born in 1816, married in 1838, in the same month as Queen Victoria was crowned, and lived until 1912, hale and hearty almost to the end. After the fashion of her day, she sat upright without cushions or footstool; she did beautiful embroidery and fancy work, and her fingers were never unoccupied. She walked out with her maid every morning and drove with my mother every afternoon, but I do not remember that she ever in my lifetime had any real business to transact, though she was always ready to help in any household matter when called upon. The delicate one of her large family, she outlived all her many brothers and sisters, though to her last days she remembered with pride that in her youth she had been sent for her health to drink the waters at Homburg. Falling down a flight of stairs when in her eighties, she merely enquired of an alarmed grandson whether her cap was straight; when the 'Tuppenny Tube' [The Central London Railway, now the Central Line, which started in 1900 using electric locomotives, Ed.] was extended to Paddington and she was nearly ninety, she ventured on the revolving staircase to see what it was like; and on her ninetieth birthday she much resented the prohibition to stand to receive her couple of hundred or more guests – all relations. Afterwards, she dined out in the evening at her son's house. I have the photo, taken when she was over seventy, which shows that she still possessed a 'waist' and the 'figure' upon which she prided herself.

I was too old to walk every afternoon with Barker and my little brother of eight and too old also to be sent to a new school. The question of continued study and matriculation therefore arose. I had no particular views or wishes, except for regular, congenial occupation and companionship, for I was lonely, unhappy and dissatisfied with my present position. My mother took all the decisions. She felt sure I should soon rebel against the prohibition to walk out by myself, and it was this that really determined my fate.

If I attended classes at Bedford College, then in Baker Street, I should, when I refused to be 'taken', have to go down Praed Street and Marylebone Road unescorted, or, equally unthinkable, journey alone by bus or underground railway. It would be far better if I could find what was needed at King's College, Ladies Department, which was situated in Kensington Square and entailed a pleasant walk of twenty minutes, mostly across Kensington Gardens. So one afternoon in the early part of October 1892, I was taken by my mother to see the Vice-Principal to make arrangements for my continued education.

How well I remember that interview with Miss Schmitz – an elegant middle-aged lady who wore a cap and had a canary bird singing above her desk in the pleasant room, looking out on a garden where she received her visitors. My mother having mentioned the word matriculation, Miss Schmitz asked me whether I knew any Latin and mathematics. Owing in part to my foreign schooling, I confessed I had never learnt either, whereupon Miss Schmitz turned to my mother saying I (just seventeen) was much too old to begin new subjects, and that in any case she strongly disapproved of examinations for girls. If my parents really desired me to pass some examination, she advised me to take correspondence courses for the Cambridge Higher Local, a test of a much higher standard than matriculation, in which I could select subjects at my own choice and, above all, be examined in one group at a time without undue stress or strain. Then I could also attend such lectures as I wished at the Ladies' Department and, most importantly, meet my father's desire for me to have drawing and painting lessons in the studio, which he considered a necessary part of a young lady's education. (He also wanted me to have cooking lessons, which I did, not at Kensington, but in a class run privately by a friend.) So my timetable was filled like a schoolgirl's, and in addition I embarked on preparation by correspondence for the Cambridge Higher Local in French and German, French and English History, English Language and Literature and Arithmetic, the last-named being compulsory for a certificate.

In 1878, King's College, London, had first given its professors permission to lecture to a group of ladies in Kensington – probably as a counterblast to the recent admission of women students to University College and the opening of London degree examinations to women candidates. From 1878 to 1885, the Kensington classes had no other connection with King's than the voluntary lectures of its professors, but in the latter year the centre was formally affiliated to the College and transferred from Observatory Avenue to Talleyrand's[35] old house at 13 Kensington Square, still in charge of Miss Schmitz, who had been responsible for the venture from the beginning and remained as Vice-Principal of the Department when it became part of King's College.

The classes were designed for the ladies, young and old, of South Kensington and Belgravia, with a smattering of the less fashionable from Bayswater, who desired to increase their knowledge by attendance at lectures. Of all ages and

---

35 Talleyrand was French ambassador to London 1830–4.

degrees of attainment, they were alike only in their sense of thwarted intellectual development and their longing for enlightenment. Much later, I well remember a pathetic old woman who was regularly carried upstairs to a lecture room, and there were many fashionable society people who seized the chance to improve themselves and make up for the deficiencies of their early education so-called. Such students did not aim at a degree or at any hallmark. Their sole desire was for culture and for the acquisition of knowledge. Even later on, when there came to be a majority of undergraduates who were preparing for professional careers, the admixture of those who worked for the love of working and with no ulterior motive remained as an inspiration to the others when they were inclined to feel weary from 'much reading'.

But when I first went to King's there were no such students and nothing remotely resembling a university or a college except the lectures of such distinguished men as S.R. Gardiner, Canon Shuttleworth, John Hales[36] and the rest. Most of the younger girls, like myself, were taken to and fetched from the classes; we did not speak to one another without formal introduction, and we had no common room or social life or societies of any kind. Nor was there provision for the study of any branch of science, or even the nucleus of a library. On the other hand, music and fine art teaching were available, though the study pursued was not 'professional'; playing, singing, painting were 'accomplishments' and so regarded by both teachers and taught, even

36 Samuel Rawson Gardiner was a noted historian of the seventeenth century; he was an extra-mural tutor for the Society for the Extension of University Teaching and taught at Toynbee Hall. Henry Cary Shuttleworth, a priest and hymn writer, was Professor of Pastoral and Liturgical Theology at King's College, London; John Wesley Hales was Professor of English Literature at King's College 1882–1903.

though the standard reached was often high, especially later on when Byam Shaw and Vicat Cole[37] took charge of the studios.

In 1894, at the end of the session, Miss Schmitz married Dr Wace, the then Principal of King's College, and in the following October we found a new young Vice-Principal, whose lines had fallen in very different places from those of her predecessor. **MISS LILIAN M. FAITHFULL** had been a scholar of Somerville, where she obtained a first class in the Honour School of English Language and Literature – at that time a women's school only. After a year as secretary to the then Principal of Somerville, **MISS SHAW-LEFEVRE**, and a year as form mistress at Oxford High School, she became lecturer in English and History at the newly founded Royal Holloway College under Miss Bishop. Then, at the age of twenty-nine, she came to King's, full of energy and determination to turn the Ladies' Department into a real women's college while retaining some of its advantages as a less stereotyped place of study. As one result, my own outlook and course of life were transformed, and, nearly fifty years on, I and my fellow students experienced many of the thrills and some of the difficulties and disappointments of the earliest women university students, the pioneers in the middle of the

---

37 Rex Vicat Cole was a landscape painter and art teacher who taught at the Women's Department of King's College, London, from 1894. In 1904 he was joined there by his friend Byam Shaw, an Indian-born artist, designer and illustrator. The two left to found the highly successful Byam Shaw and Vicat Cole School of Art in 1910.

nineteenth century. [38]

I well remember my first personal introduction to Miss Faithfull. I was still struggling with my preparation for the Cambridge Higher Local and, at that period, was engaged upon the study of Anglo-Saxon by means of correspondence lessons. In those days not even a good Anglo-Saxon grammar was available in English, and I found myself in difficulties I could not overcome. Having heard that our new Vice-Principal had been a lecturer in English, I mustered up courage to ask her help. She knew nothing of me or my capacity, but she did know that she had at last discovered someone at King's who was a student of the subject in which she was able either to provide herself or to secure adequate teaching. She rose at once to her opportunity and, my problem solved, she unhesitatingly asked me if I would like to read for the Oxford Honour School of English Language and Literature!

38 Queen's and Bedford Colleges in London, founded in the late 1840s, took girls from the age of 12 and offered a significant level of education; but it was the fight for women to train as doctors, by Elizabeth Garrett Anderson, Sophia Jex-Blake and Elizabeth Blackwell in the 1850s and 60s, which opened up the question of women's admission to degree courses. The earliest progress was made at Cambridge, where Emily Davies and Barbara Bodichon fought for the establishment of women's colleges. In Oxford the initiative was taken by the wives and daughters of college fellows; they set up the Association for the Higher Education of Women in 1878, which opened up its two first residencies, Somerville and Lady Margaret Hall, in 1879.

I should explain that women, not being members of the University – as was carefully stated on their *testamurs* [a certificate that an examination held especially by a university has been passed, Ed.] when these were gained – were at this date allowed to take Oxford University examinations of all grades, without the qualifications of residence and keeping terms. Having passed a first preliminary examination, women were also permitted to present themselves for any final Pass or Honour School without having taken Moderations, and without any question as to the length of time spent in preparation. The Oxford Women's Halls (as they then were) urged their students when possible to take the full men's courses, but many of the girls were very ill-qualified by their previous training to do so, and for these the alternative possibility was a godsend. They might even offer two modern languages instead of classics at a women's equivalent for Responsions;[39] a special pass final examination, also without compulsory Greek and Latin, was available, and various Honour Schools, e.g. in English and in Modern Languages, first came into existence for women only. That in English Language and Literature was not opened to men until 1898, the year before I took the examination. It was not until 1902 or -3 that women were obliged to go into residence at Oxford if they wished to present themselves for University examinations.

Now of all these matters I was entirely ignorant when first asked whether I should like to read for a degree examination. I knew about the Cambridge Colleges for women and had reluctantly decided long before that there was no chance for me to study there. I knew one girl who was

---

39 Responsions was an examination in Greek, Latin, Logic, and Geometry, which students had to pass before they could sit for a BA at Oxford. It was abolished in 1960.

reading science at Bedford College, but I myself had never seriously contemplated the possibility of a London degree. For one thing, there was Miss Schmitz's crushing remark about my ignorance of classics and mathematics; for another, there was the overwhelming opposition to be encountered at home. Nor had I any idea at that time of what I hoped might be the outcome of disciplined study.

I hated my then mode of existence. I found nothing to attract me to the only society open to me: dances were anathema, partly because of the shyness and gaucherie caused by over-sensitiveness about being 'fat' and having a bad figure. I hadn't enough to do, I hadn't enough companionship, and I was full of unexpressed and unformulated longings for a life of usefulness which would give me some scope for my vigour of mind and body. At the age of nineteen I found life flat, stale and unprofitable and was indeed unhappier and more discontented than ever before or since. There seemed no point in what I was doing and no way of escape into a fuller life, since no one but myself ever even contemplated the possibility or desirability of any change – unless, of course, I married and acquired a home of my own to look after.

Miss Faithfull's question came then as a complete surprise, and when she gave me an explanation of her proposal, I replied at once that I should never be allowed to accept her suggestion. She countered with another question. Did I think my mother would consent to invite her to dinner? Overjoyed and embarrassed, and immeasurably flattered, I could only stutter out that I was very sure she would be delighted to do so. The invitation given and accepted, Miss Faithfull told me not to believe a word she said to my father. She came and saw and conquered him completely by her unblushing praise of my abilities, which she had had at that time no means to estimate, nor indeed a shred of proof of their existence. By the end of dinner he would have granted any request she made on my behalf, provided it did not entail my departure from home – incidentally the last thing she desired, since she had destined me to become her pupil.

Meanwhile she had discovered more promising material in the shape of an older and much more talented young woman. **CAROLINE F. E. SPURGEON**, at that time just twenty-five years of age, seeing by chance a list of available classes outside the door, called to make enquiries about them on the very day when Miss Faithfull first arrived at Kensington Square. Miss Spurgeon at that period of her life seemed to have been visited by fairy godmothers who had endowed her with every gift. Attractive and possessed of great personal charm and a delightful speaking voice, she also excelled in everything she undertook. Thus she had exhibited in the Salon before she was twenty-one; she was so good a pianist that her masters regretted that she could not become a professional musician; she excelled in every form of athletics then open to women and had, for example, been successful at various tennis championships; and she enjoyed most forms of society entertainment. Her stepmother had done her best to curb her intellectual interests lest they might interfere with her social success, but by 1894 she had inherited a small independent income and thus became free to carry out her own plans. Her natural bents seemed to be in the direction of science or philosophy, and she had decided, after discussion with Miss Faithfull, to prepare for matriculation with a view to an ultimate course for a London BSc degree. The one subject to which she appeared at that time to feel no special attraction was that of English literature. But apart from modern languages acquired by travel in France and Italy, she had been debarred from sound school training in any branch of academic learning. Miss Faithfull soon discovered that King's College, Ladies' Department, at that date could provide no adequate preparation for a student of science or philosophy.

So having secured me as a prospective pupil in her own subject, what could be more natural than to persuade Miss Spurgeon to switch over to the same course? Somehow or other this was accomplished, and we both embarked tentatively and quite ignorantly on what were for us the uncharted seas of the Oxford Honour School of English Language and Literature.* The first session's work was pre-liminary and exploratory, but by the beginning of the session 1895–6 we were reading systematically, and we both presented ourselves for the examination in 1899, along with another girl who had spent one session at King's after a fail-ure from Somerville in the previous summer. We three were the first students of the Department to take a degree course, and with Miss Spurgeon and myself as pivots, the unrelated classes for young ladies were gradually transformed into a women's college.

Miss Faithfull remained for thirteen years as its Vice-Principal: when she left in 1907 to take up her appointment

---

* Miss Spurgeon's promise was amply fulfilled in her later career. Her contribution to Shakespearian study, notably the volume entitled *Shakespeare's Imagery* was universally acknowledged as epoch-making; her work on Chaucer criticism was outstanding and she was to become known as a leading scholar in her own subject. As University Professor of English Literature at the University of London, Bedford College for Women, she made her reputation as a great teacher, while it was also largely owing to her inspiration that the International Federation of University Women [IFUW] came into existence and acquired Crosby Hall as a centre and Club House in London.

My personal debt to her stimulus and influence during our four years of daily intercourse when undergraduates cannot be put into words, and our friendship lasted until her death, on her birthday, in October 1942.

as Principal of Cheltenham Ladies' College, there were between eighty and one hundred undergraduates in Kensington, and the Women's Department was an integral and recognised internal school of the reorganised University of London. But in the early days, practically all the regular students were secured by methods similar to those I have described. None of them was expected to earn her own livelihood or allowed to do so without a struggle. Most, if not all of them, were permitted to read for an examination only if that could be combined with taking full part in the gaieties of a London season; in some cases official attendance at classes had to be suspended during the summer term; in others a 'student' would be whisked off for the winter to Egypt or the Riviera with a sick relative or a brilliant girl would give up her hard-won chance because her conscience told her it was her duty to mother her bereaved little nieces or to look after an aged grandparent. In those early years everyone, whatever her natural bias, read for the English School at Oxford, because that was the only course for which adequate preparation could at that time be secured. But how we worked and agonised and revelled in our struggles to achieve our ambitions I think few young people can nowadays realise.

No doubt we lost very much by the need to strive for the attainment of our wish to study; no doubt that the path is much easier for those whose trail is already blazed and who have at worst only to surmount financial difficulties, serious as these often are, before they set out on their way. But I have often wondered, in intercourse with my own students, if many of them nowadays experience the thrills of adventure and fulfilled desire which were granted to us, to whom the comradeship of work and play had hitherto been unknown and to whom the disciplined training to surmount intellectual difficulties was at once a stimulus and a revelation. Be this as it may, I know I have nothing to regret and everything for which to be thankful in the fate which threw me into a struggling institution pulsing with the throbs of endeavour and purpose.

Even now, at the end of my life, I find it hard to express the extent of the debt I owe to the years that I spent at King's. Primarily, I think we attained in some small measure the power to 'live by admiration, hope and love' through our intercourse with teachers and comrades whom we justly felt to be much wiser and bigger personalities than ourselves. At the same time as we gained from these contacts, we also experienced the unfolding and development of our own capacities by our intellectual training, by coming to know something of the best thought of the best minds as it was expressed in great literature, by learning to concentrate even on uncongenial tasks, and by acquiring the power of self-expression in speech and writing.

> Youth should be awed, religiously possessed
> With a conviction of the power that waits
> On knowledge, when sincerely sought and prized
> For its own sake, on glory and on praise
> If but by labour won …
> —W. Wordsworth, *The Prelude*

With all humility I think I may claim that we were possessed with such conviction. For most of us, too, it was a new experience to work with kindred spirits in a common cause, and apart altogether from the goal of an examination, there was the daily joy of community life with all that it implied of choice of friends and fresh subjects of interest.

In her efforts to form a College out of scattered individuals attending haphazard courses of lectures, Miss Faithfull was hampered by more than the common difficulties experienced in a non-residential institution. Her students were of all ages: though some had been at Cheltenham, Roedean or Wycombe Abbey, or at a GPDS [Girls' Public Day School], most of them had received their early instruction from governesses at home or in private schools. Very few had enjoyed opportunities outside their family and social environment; almost all, young or old, had hitherto been limited by such conventions as those which forbade unmarried women to go out unescorted or to mix in any other circles than those on 'visiting terms' with their families. Unless when compelled by economic necessity, well-bred girls of their class might not earn their own living, even if openings could be found for them to do so: fathers and brothers felt it an insult to their manhood if their womenfolk suggested a 'career', and it was no uncommon argument against it that everyone would suppose that such-and-such a firm or practice must be in a bad way if Miss So-and-So had to turn out and work.

The Married Women's Property Act had become law in 1882, but many years had still to pass before it was regarded as quite suitable for young women of the well-to-do classes to enjoy economic independence. When my grandmother wished her daughters to have their own dress allowances in order that they might learn how to manage money, my grandfather vetoed the plan by saying that that was the last thing he desired his girls to know. By my day, most young women had their more or less meagre allowances and their mothers had housekeeping money as a matter of course. But very few women possessed independent incomes or even a banking account of their own. (I taught my mother how to write a cheque after my father's death in 1915, though she had always been consulted by him on all questions of ways and means.) There were still practically no women's clubs and few women's 'societies' in which they united for a common purpose. Women's athletic clubs were in their infancy, and even their charitable work was hampered by the restrictions on freedom of action.

Of course the barriers were gradually being broken down, and by the nineties of the last century, the period of which I am speaking, some of the worst obstacles had been overcome: in education, in the professions and in women's legal position.

But the Ladies Department of King's College, as Miss Faithfull found it on her arrival in 1894, was certainly not in the front line of progress, nor was it frequented by the pioneer type. On the contrary, it was ultra-respectable and proper: the 'nicest' family need not fear contamination for its daughters should they enter its doors. The question which confronted Miss Faithfull was how to retain these virtues while grafting on to them some of those advantages already experienced by herself in her career at Somerville and Royal Holloway College. In the first place, as we have seen, she determined to collect, by hook or by crook, a small nucleus of serious students prepared to undertake regular work of a university character. By means of their success at public examinations, she hoped to attract other similar students and, little by little, to widen the openings for them by enlarging the opportunities the Department and its staff could provide, and by securing recognition of those opportunities by outside academic authorities who were competent to judge.

But a College implies something more than learning and teaching, something more even than the advancement of research, which is implicit in the conception of a true University. Thus undergraduate students required the inspiration of common purpose; they needed to play as well as to work together and the life they lived must, consciously as well as sub-consciously, be adapted to the promotion of the corporate spirit, so that they could feel themselves to stand

> Upon equal ground; … brothers all
> In honour, as in one community,
> Scholars and gentlemen; ...
> —W. Wordsworth, *The Prelude*

The obvious method in such an institution as has been described was by the foundation of clubs and societies which could induce students to co-operate in ways adapted to their varied tastes and interests. We began with a Browning Society which held weekly meetings at which we read aloud and discussed Browning's poetry. These meetings were held in Miss Faithfull's drawing room, and she took an active share in them, as in all our proceedings. Herself an excellent reader and an enthusiastic admirer of Browning, she soon encouraged the shy and the ignorant to get used to the sound of their own voices in an assembly of fifteen or twenty persons. It was the business of the Secretary – a position allotted to myself – to select the poems and secure the readers in advance, and to many of these it was a new kind of obligation to keep an independently made engagement, whatever more tempting invitations might offer. The Browning Society flourished throughout my undergraduate life and for some years after: it gave us immense satisfaction and had far-reaching effects on the life of the College.

Next, a Common Room was provided in which we could meet between lectures, read or chat, or even have tea-parties on occasion. These 'socials' were great events and led to the discovery of unsuspected talent for acting, etc. A dramatic society followed, and we were lucky to find not merely that performers were available but that at least one of our number

– W. Gwyn Jeffreys[40] – could write really first-rate amateur plays. I still remember the thrill of her *Finger of Fate* and the fun we got out of its presentation. Soon we decided that our various activities demanded a record, and a magazine was started which appeared once a term. Among its earliest contributors was **EVELYN UNDERHILL**, who made her first appearance in print in its pages. The periodical was neither better nor worse than others of its kind, but it gave me, the editor, my earliest experiences of proof correction and other matters connected with publication. But far and away the most important and influential of our societies was the Hockey Club, which provided for most of us our first experience of team games and the excitement of playing for a side.

It is quite impossible to make the present generation realise what their grandmothers derived from their initiation into the joys of athletic exercise. For we had never played such games at school; the tennis we knew was a kind of patball, greatly impeded by long, voluminous skirts and tight clothing. Since we had been regarded as 'grown-up', we had been discouraged from running or other forms of violent exercise. Many of us (though this was not so in my own case) had never been allowed to take long walks, to climb over walls, to get wet feet or indulge in any similar unladylike performances. If we could afford to ride – a pleasure beyond my own means – we mounted our horses in flowing habits and could not get on or off the saddle unaided. We were unsuitably clad for any and every exercise and were therefore perpetually instructed that women's bodies were not adapted by nature to strenuous exertion. Nor had it altogether ceased to be considered a mark of refinement to be 'delicate' and to

40 Winifred Gwyn Jeffreys was for 17 years secretary to the poet John Drinkwater. A production of *The Finger of Fate* was also performed in 1946 in Winter Park, Florida.

possess feet and hands that were disproportionately small and correspondingly useless, and many of us had been taught to 'take care of our complexions' by seeing that they were not exposed to wind and rain. Thus tremendous home opposition often had to be overcome before permission could be gained to indulge in so unfeminine a pastime, though I personally encountered few or no such difficulties. But I well recall that while a bruise on the leg, or elsewhere not visible to the public eye, caused no trouble, most of the players dreaded a blow on the face lest it should result in prohibitions to play in future. On one occasion I recall a search for raw beefsteak with which to prevent the development of a black eye. We asked at a cottage, where the puzzled servant girl, seeing two well-fed and hefty young women, had nothing better to offer as a panacea than 'cold Irish stew' which was not accepted by my injured companion.

The King's College Club was amongst the earliest London hockey clubs for women, though it was not the first, and the game had been played for ten years or more at women's residential colleges. But the sight of a hockey stick in a girl's hands was sufficiently unusual for passers-by or bus conductors to subject her to cries of 'new woman', and we were at first all very self-conscious when on our way to and from Wormwood Scrubs, where the King's College ground was situated, in the neighbourhood of the prison. We were inordinately proud of our uniform, which I am afraid would nowadays be regarded as both unsuitable and funny. Our skirts (under which petticoats were actually discarded) of navy blue serge had to be six inches off the ground. Since this was felt to be unduly short, it was not unusual for them to be rather longer, so that the captain often went round the team with a tape-measure to see that the rule was obeyed. We all of us changed into these skirts for the game only, as we should have been ashamed to appear in anything so indecently short except on the playing-field. Our blouses were of soldier-red flannel; our long ties of red and blue stripes. We wore high, starched white collars and tight belts, and blue 'boater'-shaped straw hats with a ribbon of the King's College colours (red and blue) and the lion and crown crest in front. Hats were not usually worn for play, and in no case were hatpins permitted![*]

Miss Faithfull's method of collecting players resembled her ways of obtaining examination candidates. Anyone became a student of King's by enrolling herself for a single course of lectures for a whole or even a half term. The cheapest lectures were those in Divinity, since this was a compulsory subject for matriculated undergraduates at King's College, a Church of England foundation. Consequently prospective hockey players without intellectual leanings were, I regret to say, encouraged to pay for a half term's course of Divinity lectures, I think at the cost of 5/3d., in order that they could become entitled to rank as students of King's and therefore to join the Hockey Club. No-one enquired whether such 'casuals' attended the instruction they had paid for, and I fear that they did not always profit by it in any other way than by the right to play for the College.

---

[*] In 1901 I was a member of the first English women's hockey team to play in Holland – not of course an international team such as came later into existence – and went annually to play the Dutch. This experience of the beginnings of continental hockey for women was great fun, and from the time of arrival at Haarlem station, where we were sorted out by our several hostesses, we enjoyed every minute of it. But the Dutch girls at that period did wear hats skewered on with pins; they also played vigorously with a large bouncing yellow ball, about twice the size of an English one. At first, especially at the 'mixed' practices in the mornings, we went in terror of the consequences. Luckily nothing untoward occurred and we won all our matches, at one of which Queen Wilhelmina was a spectator. I was never a good player, though a most enthusiastic one, and I count it a piece of great luck to have had this thrilling experience.

In this fashion we secured some of our foremost players and notably our captain, **LILIAN CLAPHAM**. Like Miss
Faithfull, she was not only a keen player, but also deeply
interested in the formation of the All England Women's
Hockey Association, which was in process of creation at this
period[*] and of which Miss Faithfull was the first President.
Women's county teams were coming into being, and King's
was soon proud to have members playing for Middlesex and
Surrey, and later, in the person of Miss Clapham, to provide
the captain of the English International Eleven. Another of
our members, Edith Thompson,[†] was responsible for starting, off her own bat and quite without journalistic experience, *The Hockey Field*, the paper which she edited until 1914
and which was, and I believe still is, the official organ of the
Association. Matches were a recurring and perpetual excitement in the two winter terms, and one with which nothing
was allowed to interfere. I still remember Mr (afterwards
Professor) de Sélincourt's expression of astonishment when
I politely and in all innocence explained to him that it was
impossible for Miss Spurgeon and me to come to his tutorial on a certain afternoon when it happened to clash with
an important fixture. To us the excuse appeared perfectly
valid. But as he came specially from Oxford to lecture in the

---

[*]   It has recently [1945] celebrated its Jubilee.

[†]   Edith M. Thompson CBE later did yeoman service as second in
     command of the WAAC [Women's Army Auxiliary Corps] during
     the First World War. In the recent war she was attached to the High
     Commissioner's Office in Pretoria (the first woman to hold such a
     position) to look after the British women and children evacuated
     to South Africa. She was one of the majority of her contemporaries
     at King's College, Women's Department, who read for no degree
     examination. Nevertheless she has had a varied and outstanding
     career, to the notable success of which her humour and common sense
     have contributed almost as much as her unusual ability.

morning and to coach us after lunch, his surprise was perhaps not so strong as we considered it.

It was the Hockey Club which cemented our closest friendships and gave us a real sense of belonging to a corporate body. Even those of us to whom our work was of outstanding importance, as it certainly was to Cara Spurgeon and myself, would unhesitatingly have declared that what we learned and derived from playing together was of almost equal value in our education. Looking back after all these years, I am inclined to think we were right, and that the training in sportsmanship in its widest sense indeed contributed something to our development which girls with our individualistic upbringing could have got in no other way from a non-residential college. Apart from the actual game, there were by-products of the Club which were also good fun and hitherto unknown to us. For example, there was the Annual Hockey Dinner, for which a curious assortment of food and drink was collected from our parents, together with the loan of crockery, etc. These dinners were conducted in the manner of public functions and were followed by toasts and speeches – the first we had ever made or heard. College songs were composed and sung with great fervour, and we were convinced that no other College was 'as happy as King's'.

The reference to speech-making reminds me of the College Parliament, where many of us learned for the first time to take a serious interest in political matters. Its procedure was closely modelled on that of the House of Commons and we debated with vigour most of the questions of the day.

These things must appear commonplace and ordinary to young people who have grown up at schools where they have had similar opportunities since childhood. But I want to emphasise that for us, grown women of all ages, they provided something totally new in our experience, something enlarging to the spirit as well as to the mind. For by their means we began to find ourselves, and to feel ourselves responsible people, with interests not necessarily shared by our families and with points of view that were our own and independently formed.

The Bicycle Club was not started till 1897, the year when bicycling became a fashionable society pastime, and Battersea Park a rendezvous which rivalled Rotten Row[41] in popularity. My own bicycle was acquired a year sooner, a twenty-first birthday present from an uncle who gave it me the spring before I attained my majority so that I could use it during the summer months. A few women had begun to ride a year or so before when safety bicycles first came into use, but in 1896 bicycling was still so unusual a proceeding for girls, that my father took counsel with various medical friends to find out whether there was any likelihood of my injuring myself permanently if he allowed me to accept the proffered gift.

The acceptance of that bicycle marks an epoch in my life for it brought me, as it brought many other girls, hitherto undreamed-of freedom and emancipation. The bicycle meant the speedy end of chaperonage, the power to go on long expeditions on one's own, the means of locomotion and enterprise previously denied to women. We rode, as we did everything else, in wholly unsuitable garments – skirts, braided as usual round the hem, but only four yards wide instead of the customary seven; gaiters to the knee, lest too much leg were exposed; tight underclothes; hats secured by dangerously protruding pins – but we rode: into the country,

41 Rotten Row is a bridle path running through Hyde Park from Hyde Park Corner to the Serpentine Road. It was a fashionable place for riding in the nineteenth century. Established by William III at the end of the seventeenth century, it was called *Route du Roi* (King's Road), which may have become corrupted in due course to Rotten Row.

in the busy streets, to and from engagements made independently with our own friends. We even went away on holiday with other girls, abroad as well as at home. Thus the first summer I possessed a bicycle we spent a month at Bowness, and it took nearly the whole of that period to persuade my father to allow me to ride thence to Brighton, alone with a brother of nineteen, sleeping at hotels en route. The following year I made my first foreign bicycling tour in France with a couple of other women – one of them, it is true, a youngish widow and therefore supposed competent to act as chaperone. But we were unescorted – and this is the noteworthy point – by any man or any older female relative, and this time permission had been easy to gain.* For meanwhile other girls had also obtained the key of the street through the possession of bicycles and it was becoming less and less unusual for them to be seen about alone.

Yet only a very few years before, when two young women of twenty-three and twenty-five were invited with their older brother to my coming-out dance, they were

---

* This was the forerunner of many tours at home and abroad. On that first occasion we crossed to Caen, and our itinerary took us to all the places which first figured on the war maps after D-day – inter alia Bayeux, Balleroy, St Lô and Coutances. But our thoughts were far from war as we rode through the quiet Norman and Breton villages, made tea by the roadside and distributed used tea-leaves among eager peasants, admired cathedrals or scenery and generally enjoyed our experiences. There was a later expedition when we explored the Meuse, Moselle and Rhine and got into trouble for coasting downhill with feet up, in days when free-wheels were not yet invented. This was 'strengstens verboten', but when called to order by a policeman, we untruthfully shouted 'verstehen kein deutsch' and proceeded apace. Luckily his sword and spurs, as well has his inability to follow our example, impeded his progress, for we discovered later that our transgression was punishable by six weeks imprisonment. On that same tour in Germany every man, woman and child shouted 'All Heil' to bicyclists as they passed. We had to take it in turn to respond to the greeting, of which we got heartily sick, well meant as it doubtless was.

not allowed to accept unless accompanied by their mother. This was not altogether exceptional. My own father was at first rather horrified at the idea that I should go to parties, escorted by an older brother and in my grandmother's carriage, unless my mother came with us. Luckily she was on our side in this matter, and my father – already rather old-fashioned in his ideas of what was seemly – compromised on condition she went with us to dances not held in private houses but in public halls – a rare occurrence in those days.

Poor man, he had to get used to much of which he disapproved in my behaviour, and it was lucky for me that he usually first tolerated and then condoned and even sanctioned my proceedings, because everything I did sooner or later somehow came to be justified in his eyes. It is true that by modern standards I did nothing either shocking or even unusual, but, as I have said, he was very conservative, not merely in politics, and I rode rough-shod over all the conventions he respected, let alone those of my own contemporaries. It must have caused him a pang to give me a latchkey as he did for my twenty-first birthday. I am writing now at the roll-top office desk with which, at my request, he also presented me on that occasion, though he considered it quite unsuited to a young lady's requirements. He denied me nothing that I said was requisite for my education or for my pleasure, but he could not have liked to see me smoke, and only my sex could make him regard my reprehensible political views as negligible. Generally, my conduct did not conform to his code of the proprieties either in what I did or what I left undone.

Nor was my mother in much better case with regard to my proceedings, though in much more sympathy with my intellectual leanings. These facts need emphasis because they were harder to face and overcome than violent or obstinate opposition. It is comparatively easy to contend with mere unreason and antagonism, but extremely hard to fight those whose love is proven and unquestionable and whose only motive is obviously the promotion of what they believe to be one's well-being. We hear a great deal nowadays of women's earlier struggle against their opponents for their rights and their freedom.[42] Less is said concerning the more painful and pain-giving necessity of contention with parents, brothers and friends about the countless little things which, in their sum, created a mountain of difficulty and repression.

I still believe that we were justified in our battle for liberty, but it was not fought and won without heart-searchings and unhappiness for victors as well as vanquished. Nor is it surprising that some of the fighters became unnecessarily aggressive and dogmatic in manner, or that they lost some of the feminine qualities it would have been better and happier for them to retain, even from the point of view of the cause they were championing. These things were temporarily inevitable and part of the price paid for victory – in many cases consciously and with regret, in others without recognition of what had been abandoned in the course of the conflict. But I know that many who were supposed to 'enjoy a good fight' in fact – from a sheer sense of duty – trained themselves deliberately and unwillingly to the contest.

Let us return from this digression to my intellectual training. Miss Faithfull acted most efficiently as tutor to Miss Spurgeon and myself, and she was a most stimulating and admirable teacher. She also lectured regularly at least once a week, but it soon became necessary to provide other

42 Mary Wollstonecraft's *Vindication of the Rights of Women* (1792) is perhaps the founding text for feminism. In the 1830s and 40s the Unitarians fought for legal and civil rights for women, and their aims were taken up in the 1850s by such women as Barbara Bodichon, Bessie Rayner Parks and Josephine Butler.

instruction, especially on the linguistic side. Among the teachers she secured for us was Dr (later Sir) Gregory Foster, then a young man at the beginning of his career, a lecturer at Bedford College and an assistant at University College, of which later on he was to become the first Provost. Almost as soon as he made our acquaintance and heard of our plans, Dr Foster began to persuade us to attend Professor Ker's lectures at University College: we ought not to miss the chance of instruction from one of the greatest scholars and greatest men we were ever likely to meet. We were fired by his enthusiasm, broached the scheme to Miss Faithfull and obtained her rather unwilling consent. Though eager to obtain for us the best attainable assistance at King's, she would have preferred us not to work at another college.

However, in January 1897 to University College we went as what would nowadays be called 'inter-collegiate' students, and we had the inestimable benefit of attending Professor Ker's lectures and classes until we took Schools [final examinations, Ed.] in June 1899, and subsequently as post-graduate students. W.P. Ker was the greatest scholar I have known, the greatest intellectual force and stimulus in my own life as in that of a multitude of others. Not particularly gifted as a teacher, since he could not envisage the elementary difficulties of the ignorant or tolerate the stupid or lazy, he nevertheless inspired and aroused all those who were in the least capable of appreciating his learning, the width and depth of his wisdom, his dry humour and sarcasm.[*]

---

[*] It is worthwhile to reprint an oft told and typical story of him. He was walking one day with a friend who asked the name of a bird which they passed. 'A woodcock,' said W.P.K. 'It's not my idea of a woodcock', replied the other. 'It's God's idea of a woodcock', rejoined W.P.K. [According to R.W. CHAMBERS, in a lecture on King Lear, this is the 'deplorable woodcock heresy' and the bird in question was a magpie. Ed.]

I think we sensed the magnanimity of soul behind his hatred of slackness and inefficiency. Certainly we derived from him very much besides the knowledge of books – not least important, perhaps, the conviction that good work, even in unobserved details, was essential to right living and an index of moral rectitude. His lectures were delivered, apparently extemporarily, very slowly, quietly and with frequent pauses. In fact they must have been most carefully prepared, as may be proved by a comparison between courses given in different years. The later versions closely resemble or develop out of the earlier treatment of the same subjects, and there can be no doubt of the amount of thought and work put into them before delivery. Not a word is wasted: every epithet is needed to bring out the particular point, and the matter is so close-packed that often a single sentence or paragraph might well suggest sufficient substance for an hour's talk by a lesser man.

Certainly his unemphatic voice and manner conveyed to us a sense of his mastery, and his constant references to and long quotations from writers in many languages, ancient and modern, made us realise the continuity of literature as an indivisible and vital human force. For him no barriers of time or place or language were insuperable. Just as he refused to recognise any dividing line between 'literature' and 'language', so too he laid stress always on the unity of human culture, each part of which contributed to a living whole. In those days, when the science of philology was still fighting rather aggressively for domination in university schools of English, W. P. Ker was amongst the earliest to emphasise that, since language was the medium of literature, students needed knowledge of both aspects of their subject at all stages if they were to be competent to appreciate and to criticise the masters of style.

Today, when that truth is more generally accepted, Ker's methods of dealing with 'set books' do not appear so revolutionary as they seemed in my undergraduate days. But they are rare teachers who are equally competent both to illuminate by a phrase or comment a philosophical thought or historical allusion, draw attention to poetic achievement, or solve a difficult crux, and to give an explanation of a grammatical or semantic development or make intelligible a linguistic emendation or philological point. We sometimes found his expositions of texts dull: but we had the sense to attend such classes even when he dealt with books not set for our own examination. I know now what I was not then fully competent to grasp: how great a wealth of learning went into his slow and careful commentary.

His lectures were in another category altogether, and there was no mistaking their value, or the intellectual stimulus to be derived from them. This seemed to be generally appreciated, for in the Higher Senior Class[43] during the period I attended it, he had collected a surprising number of students who were later to make names for themselves, among whom **R. W. CHAMBERS, ALLEN MAWER** (then a post-graduate from Cambridge who attended the Old Norse classes) and Caroline Spurgeon were outstanding but by no means alone.

During our last long vacation, in July 1898, Miss Faithfull took us for a week's reading to Somerville College, where she worked us hard and also spent much time teaching us to scull and to manage a boat. While we were in Oxford, we looked about on our own account for good coaching in our language work and were lucky enough to persuade Miss Wardale, Mrs Wright and Miss M. L. Lee to consent to give us help by correspondence. Miss Faithfull also arranged for the last named to come to King's once a week during our final session, and I can confidently assert that it was mainly due to her teaching that we ever succeeded in reaching the

43 Over a two or three year course students were divided into junior and senior classes (or years) each with a lower and higher division.

requisite standard in our linguistic studies. She threw light on what had been dark places, filled up the many gaps in our knowledge, and made us grasp for the first time the meaning, coherence and use of philological study. Miss Lee was far and away the best language teacher we had met, and both as undergraduate and later, for many years, as a colleague I owed an inestimable debt to her scholarly methods and example. One other tremendous privilege of our undergraduate lives requires mention, especially as it derived from what might have been a hopeless situation. We had no library at King's College, Women's Department (a new name which indicated new beginnings)[44] – at first not even dictionaries, reference books and grammars. Gradually and slowly we built up a small collection of a few thousand, but in my student days there were no books at all. Quite early in our career we discovered Dr Williams's[45] Library in Gordon Square, that inestimable legacy and foundation of the early eighteenth-century nonconformist minister who 'showed by one satiric touch' the noblest means of revenge on those who excluded him and his co-religionists from attendance at British universities. His library, open free to all who are in need of books, is a lasting monument of tolerance and charity.

Then, by **DR FURNIVALL**'s mediation, long before I attained my majority, as was normally required, I obtained entry to the British Museum Reading Room. There Miss Spurgeon and I regularly resorted and discovered for

---

44 King's College Ladies Department was renamed King's College Women's Department in 1902. In 1910 it became King's College for Women.

45 Dr Daniel Williams left his library of about 7600 volumes for the benefit of fellow non-conformist ministers. Although he also left some money, further funds had to be raised in order to purchase a building which opened in 1729, some 13 years after his death. The Library is still in existence, the collections relating mainly to non-conformity, plus an impressive collection of manuscripts.

ourselves, happily and without guidance, how to select the books we needed for the composition of our essays and for general study.

We caused a good deal of amusement to the authorities in the process[*] for to begin with we had no notion of selection, but attempted, when it was not obviously impossible (as e.g. in the case of Shakespeare) to look at everything that had been written about a particular author or subject. Of course we wasted much time and labour, but we learned how to find what we needed and, I still think, derived immeasurable benefit from our efforts – far greater than could have accrued from reading only what had been chosen by a librarian or advised by our teachers.

As we could take our time and had no terms to keep, there was very much to be said for this unusual means of preparing for an examination. I am sure we managed to cover much more ground than the ordinary undergraduate, not because we wished to do so, but because we knew no other way. And because no other method seemed possible, we read the historians, philosophers and divines whose names occurred in the annals of literature, so that we were not limited to the men-of-letters proper but went far beyond the scope of any syllabus. No doubt we suffered from literary indigestion in consequence, but I for one have never regretted the effects of an over-rich diet at a time when I was eager to assimilate everything I could come by. At no other period of my life have I enjoyed equal opportunities for quiet rumination and adventurous prospecting among books, nor would I have

---

[*] We also derived some fun from them. There was for example the occasion when we overheard a delightful wrangle between Edmund Gosse and one of the men at the centre desk. An irritable complaint about the delay in supplying books ended with the supposedly unanswerable statement: 'I am Edmund Gosse'. 'And who is Mr Edmund Gosse?' came the crushing rejoinder.

wanted it any different for myself, whatever may be normally more suitable.

I must not forget another favourite opportunity of making the acquaintance of various editions and authors known and unknown. The second-hand dealers in Charing Cross Road, St Martin's Lane and elsewhere were our frequent resort, and we profited greatly by our researches, not merely by unearthing sundry treasures or what we so regarded, but also by acquiring considerable information. There were not many reprints of English classics in those days which were within the means of an impecunious student, and it was a triumph in more ways than one to dig out an early edition and carry it off for a few pence. I well remember trudging home from Red Lion Square on one occasion with two folio volumes under my arm – Swift's edition of Temple's works with several aquatints, which I had picked up for 2/- and could not wait to have delivered. I felt myself to be a true disciple of Charles Lamb which doubtless counterbalanced the weight of the parcel!

We had not been allowed to become matriculated students of King's College at the beginning of our course, a privilege not granted to women at that time. But after we had taken our examination at Oxford, the Council, spurred on by the then Principal, Dr Robertson, later Bishop of Exeter, offered to bestow on us the Associateship of King's College. Naturally we accepted this honour with pleasure, especially as we had no other letters to put after our names.[*] But as a preliminary, now at the conclusion of our undergraduate

---

[*] Women who took Oxford or Cambridge Honours examinations did not gain degrees as the result of their success but were said to have 'obtained the equivalent'. Consequently many women from the old universities subsequently took pass degrees at London in order to be able to call themselves BA or BSc Then in 1901 Trinity College, Dublin, being in financial straits, conceived the idea of awarding *ad eundem* degrees [courtesy degrees awarded by one university or college to the alumni of another, Ed.] to such women as had kept their terms and taken the full course at Oxford or Cambridge. Large numbers of women obtained

career, we had first to become matriculated students, to whom alone the Associate of King's College could be awarded. I still grudge the guinea it cost me more than any similar sum I have been obliged to expend in the course of my life.

these Dublin degrees in that and the following year, when the concession came to an end. In 1920, when women were first admitted to full membership of the University of Oxford, degrees were of course thrown open to them. At Cambridge, where membership of the University is still not conceded, women graduates are now permitted to use the titles of the degrees they have obtained. Miss Spurgeon and I were anxious to obtain degrees but were excluded from so doing by a variety of reasons. Professor Ker wished us to take a London MA on the strength of our Oxford 'equivalent to a degree', but after we had already started our proposed theses, our application for permission to do so was rejected because we had not taken Greek at Oxford which was still obligatory for a London BA, though it ceased to be so in the following year. Dublin would not look at us because we had not been in residence at Oxford, and for the same reason Oxford naturally would not give us degrees when these were thrown open and ex-students of the women's colleges at the University were granted them retrospectively (often only after the completion of some minor examination such as Divinity which had been omitted by them when undergraduates). Ultimately, Miss Spurgeon went to Paris, where she obtained a brilliant *doctorat de l'Université* at the Sorbonne for her book entitled *Chaucer devant la Critique.* But I had no time or money to take a foreign degree.

After the last war it became customary for senior teachers in the University of London to submit work for a doctorate of that University. But I had severed my connection with it in 1914 so was no longer eligible. It was not till February 1926 that Oxford conferred on me a degree *honoris causa*, and at last I had the right to call myself MA, and of the University to which I was proudest to belong. Meanwhile King's College for Women had bestowed on both Miss Spurgeon and myself the Fellowship of the College. It may be thought that the absence of the right to a hood and to letters after one's name is a small matter in comparison with the enjoyment of a university education. So indeed it is, but it is nevertheless the cause of annoyance and pin-pricks of various kinds in academic life, and it is much easier to possess, unquestioned, the same status as one's male colleagues who, presumably, invented it because it was thought to be a convenience. It may be noted that it is still very rare for an honorary doctorate to be conferred on a woman, and the exceptions are most frequently not in recognition of purely academic work.

CHAPTER 5

First years of professional work

At the beginning of the following term, in October 1899, when my future plans were still quite unsettled, Miss Faithfull unexpectedly offered me some tutorial work at the Ladies' Department, and I began my teaching career with a class in Gothic and Germanic Philology, my pupils being some six or eight friends who had been my fellow students the previous term. I also coached the first London BA candidate we had in Kensington, Kathleen Robinson, in her English work, and another girl who was reading for an Irish degree, Charlotte Houston.

When this opening was presented to me, I was still encountering a good deal of opposition at home to my intention to teach. For some inexplicable reason, however, my father thought it more exalted to become a college lecturer than a high school mistress, and he made no difficulties about the acceptance of the work offered to me, so that I entered on my professional life with nothing to dampen my enthusiasm except natural fears about my competence and possession of the requisite tact. With my parents I had already concluded a pact which was honourably observed to the end. They had promised to treat me exactly like my brothers, to make no further difficulties about my complete freedom of action and to raise no objections to my future doings or omissions: on these conditions I undertook for my part to continue to make home my headquarters and not to accept a post which made it impossible for me to do so.

This agreement was of lasting influence on my career, as to a large extent it determined where I was to work. My parents consented to it very unwillingly and, I feel sure, only with great pain. But I know also that the fact of the given word prevented subsequent disputes and bickerings and made it possible for us all three to get the best out of each other and to live in harmony. It also enabled me so to arrange my affairs that I could care for them in their old age without the unnecessary sacrifice of my professional work. Whether as a result of my own experience or not, it has always been an article of faith with me that the young should not be called upon to subordinate their work as citizens to the older generation, nor have I ever been able to acquiesce in the once universally accepted assumption that an unmarried woman must give up all her own interests in order to tend her aged relatives.

In my youth, every hotel was full of old people, each with a young woman in attendance, and it has always seemed to me that it is wrong and unnecessary so to organise society that the elderly must become a burden instead of an inspiration to their juniors. At any rate, by the exercise of judicious firmness, I succeeded in my own case in making it possible to combine my work with the requisite care of my parents, and once the matter was settled, I do not think that either they or I had cause to regret that we had come to an understanding on the subject before my temper was soured by the lack of congenial and useful occupation and my prospects of happiness thereby blighted. I am convinced that the benefit was not all on my side, but that they derived equal profit from the fact that I was gladly instead of grudgingly at their service when they came to need my care.

When I first became a tutor at King's College, Ladies' Department, no woman member of the teaching body except the Vice-Principal was appointed by the Council and on the regular academic staff of the College. That followed a few years later when I, as well as my senior colleagues, became recognised lecturers of both the College and the newly organised teaching University of London. Meanwhile many other changes had gradually take place in the position of the Women's Department. It had soon become obvious that a college could not continue to offer only one course of study to its regular students; nor could a London institution limit its examination work to preparation for an Oxford Honour School. So while the group of English students continued until the Oxford Schools were closed to non-resident women, I think in 1903, Miss Faithfull turned her attention to the provision of facilities in other subjects for all stages of the University of London degree examinations.

Science laboratories were established in Chemistry, Physics and Botany in which students – now allowed to matriculate – could work up to the Intermediate standard. This first-year examination surmounted, the science students proceeded to the parent college in the Strand for Final and Higher work, in those and some other subjects. At first the women were not allowed to compete for prizes at King's, but this embargo was lifted after one historic occasion when the results read out showed a woman in the first place in Chemistry, Botany and Physiology, in each of which subjects the prize was awarded to a man whose name was below her in the lists. The anomaly was too glaring to continue, and henceforward men and women competed on equal terms – of course by no means usually with similar results, though at first the women candidates were all picked, and therefore normally very much above the average. Helen Fraser (now **PROFESSOR DAME HELEN GWYNNE VAUGHAN**) was, for example, the abovementioned successful botany student. Henrietta Tayler, one of the others, and now well known as the Jacobite historian, was typical of our King's women. She took no public examination, but read up to examination standard in various subjects as different as English and Physiology, from sheer interest and in order to share the pursuits of her friends. Such students contributed greatly by their genuine love of knowledge to the tone of the Department as a centre of learning.

About the turn of the century, Miss Faithfull secured the gift of an entrance scholarship from the Merchant Taylors' Company, and soon after we began to enrol students who came to prepare for professional careers. Among the earliest were G.M. Harcourt-Smith, our first scholar, who was *proxime accessit* [runner up, Ed.] for the George Smith scholarship[46] at her BA examination, ultimately obtained first class honours in English, and subsequently took her MA with distinction, and L. Meyer, who got a first class honours in History at her BA examination. The Department was still woefully poor and hampered by a lack of means. The next step was to secure a certain influx of regular undergraduate students, which was accomplished by the admittance of what were then known as Technical Education Board scholars – girls who were in receipt of a training grant in preparation for the teaching profession. This meant great changes in the life of the College and a mixture of social classes which proved to be beneficial to all concerned.

Miss Faithfull determined that all matriculated students should enjoy as far as possible the advantages of the Oxford tutorial system and, speaking as the chief tutor to arts students, I am convinced of her wisdom in instituting this method of supervision – an innovation at that date in any of the newer universities and colleges. Teachers and taught alike benefited from the closer intimacy engendered, and the results in both work and character were in all respects satisfactory. It became possible to influence one's pupils in countless directions, and to obtain their confidence and give them help which could not otherwise have been offered. In many

---

46 Awarded annually by the University of London for the person with the highest marks in BA English.

instances the resulting friendships were of lasting value to both parties, and I know that my own life would have been much poorer had I lacked this experience and opportunity in my early professional years.[*]

The development and growth of the internal teaching – as distinct from the external, purely examining side – of the University of London brought about many changes in King's College, Women's Department, as in all the constituent schools of the University. The outward sign for undergraduates in Kensington was the wearing of academic dress, of which the students were immensely proud. Their teachers also acquired new functions and duties, among them the privilege of taking their share in the shaping of University policy and the conduct of University examinations at all stages. Those considered suitable became 'recognised' teachers of the University and members of the appropriate Boards of Study and Faculty.

As far as I was concerned, this gave me my first insight into university administration and policy discussion, and I derived immense benefit from mixing on equal terms with my seniors, listening to their opinions and, at times, venturing to give my own. It was also a very valuable experience to have a share in the framing of syllabuses and in the work of the Board of Examiners. Later on, the setting and correction of examination papers came to be the least agreeable part of university teaching, but in those early years of professional life the tedium was easily outweighed by the excitement of learning from one's betters how to judge, appraise and mark fairly. It required some considerable effort to hold my own against some of my co-examiners, and I well remember my fears when I first had to be responsible for setting and correcting an honours paper with such a colleague as Professor Ker, **PROFESSOR HERFORD** (one of my own examiners) or →

[*] Cf. p.110/11 for an account of the similar system at Reading.

PROFESSOR GOLLANCZ (then Professor of English at King's College, to whom I was therefore directly subordinate as a lecturer on its academic staff).

At my age and to anyone of my standing such experience would necessarily have been awe-inspiring as well as instructive, but I think I am right in believing that the unquestioned admission of women to all university governing bodies was, at that time, epoch-making, in that it had never previously occurred at any British university. For my seniors as well as for myself it was a new recognition of equality, and the University of London was once more establishing a precedent by opening its official bodies to both sexes on equal terms. At any rate, Miss Faithfull gave all her women colleagues a little homily on the responsibility incurred by acceptance of a place on a committee, and upon the need for punctual and regular attendance at meetings and taking due but not excessive part in any discussion that might ensue. For in those days women were very apt to hold their tongues even when they had something worthwhile to contribute, because they were frightened to intervene or to put themselves forward when men were present. It is only right and just to add that, neither in those early days or later, have I ever found any reluctance by male colleagues to listen to a woman who had any views to express or argument to sustain. On the contrary, they usually appear to resent silence and lack of participation that are obviously caused by undue shrinking from public speech.

King's College, Women's Department, necessarily remained a very small 'school' of the University, being constrained by lack of funds for expansion and by entirely inadequate premises, which consisted only of two private houses. There was indeed but one lecture room which could hold an audience of fifty or sixty people; there was no hall for assemblies or functions; most of the classrooms were poky and small; there were no adequate common rooms; etc. etc. If, as we hoped, King's was to serve the west side of London, as Bedford College catered for the centre, it was clear that new premises must be acquired. Our students often journeyed in from as far west as Richmond, Hounslow and Wimbledon, or even further afield: there seemed no doubt the Department had a function to fulfil if the means could be found.

One entirely new development had already been inaugurated, which was felt to be peculiarly suited to a Church foundation. This was the undertaking to prepare students for the Diploma in Theology for Women, which had recently been established by Archbishop Davidson, the friend of our Vice-Principal. The Theological Faculty of King's College was able to provide the requisite tuition, and the Women's Department became the centre for the new venture, which at once attracted a small but deeply interested group of students. Miss Faithfull's next idea was of a very different kind, and one which seemed likely to have wide repercussions on women's education in general and our own position in particular.

When girls gradually won their way to school and university education, they had first to convince themselves and their opponents that they could profit by the same curriculum and training as the other sex. Their primary business was to prove that their minds were equal to the study of subjects which had hitherto been regarded as beyond their grasp. So the new schools for girls were modelled as closely as possible on those for boys, and when, step by step, university training and examinations were opened to women, there was no thought of asking for anything different for them than was provided for their brothers.

It was natural that early women students should all have been 'picked' people, for only those who possessed unusual ability and unusual persistence in attaining their purpose were ever likely to get to university at all after years of struggle and disappointment. When the chance at last came, they had no desire to idle or to waste their opportunities: for themselves as individuals and for all other women, everything depended on their success in the courses of study and the examinations which had been primarily designed for the needs of men. Thus there gradually grew up a lamentable division in girls' schools between those who were likely to succeed at academic pursuits and those whose interests lay elsewhere. Nor is it unknown, even at the present time, that only the 'unintelligent' are relegated to the 'domestic side' while the others confine themselves at school to the usual examination subjects.

In post-school training it had been discovered, long before the beginning of this century, that there was an important place for the proper teaching of the domestic arts. However, owing to the abovementioned school bias, the pupils who entered the Domestic Training Colleges were at first often not distinguished by intelligence or by adequate school preparation. They sometimes took up their work only because they were considered below the average in book-learning, just as those girls held to be too stupid to become clerks or junior civil servants were, and still are, often relegated to domestic service. This absurd and reprehensible point of view has had many evil results, and I suppose that nowadays no-one would seriously challenge the assertion that it requires at least as much (though not the same kind of) ability to run a house, to bring up and feed a family properly, as to engage in any other occupation, and that these things are no more successfully undertaken by the stupid or ignorant than anything else. Further, the underlying sciences of dietetics, cooking, laundry work, etc. are as necessary a study for the trained housewife as they are for the agriculturalist or technician.

At any rate, Miss Faithfull, eagerly backed by members of her Committee of Management, notably LADY (CARL) MEYER, LADY (ARTHUR) RUCKER and by her friends MISS S.T. PRIDEAUX and MRS MCKILLOP (lecturer in Chemistry and Mathematics), conceived the idea of instituting a degree course leading to a BSc in domestic subjects. This was to combine a thorough study of the appropriate branches of science and economics with a certain amount of practical cooking, housewifery, etc. It was not intended to replace the usual Domestic College training and was designed to follow or precede fuller practice of the domestic arts. The degree was to meet the needs of the scientific investigator into domestic problems, the teacher, the matron, large-scale caterer, dietician, etc. The course as planned was, if anything, over-full and certainly in no sense a soft option as compared with other undergraduate curricula. It was an integral part of the scheme that the BSc (Domestic Science) students should form a faculty or group which shared fully in the life of the College of which they were to be a part: from every point of view it was felt to be desirable that they should not be segregated. Their degree was to have full University status: they themselves ought to have the benefit of working on a par with and among undergraduates who were pursuing a variety of subjects, and so derive one of the great advantages of university life: the sense of community in diversity of interests, and the conviction that while there are many different paths by which it may be sought, the single goal of learning is the discovery of truth.

With characteristic energy, Miss Faithfull set about her new task. The first step was to clear off the debt on the existing buildings, which was somehow accomplished; the next to find a suitable site and secure the necessary endowment and money for the new College. The preliminary work was completed when a site on Campden Hill was found and plans made for its development. The idea of a degree for women in Domestic Science caught on even among those who were opposed to or uninterested in women's higher education in other subjects: support and money began to come in, and it looked as if the scheme would mature and the College come into existence. Then the blow fell. In the summer of 1907, Miss Faithfull accepted the appointment of Principal of Cheltenham Ladies College and left King's College, Women's Department, in order to take up her new work.

Her successor in Kensington, **MISS HILDA OAKELEY**, was of a very different type. A scholar to the fingertips, she was among the earliest women to obtain a first class in the Oxford *Lit. Hum.* examination. She is a distinguished philosopher and no-one could come in close contact with her, either as a colleague or student, without being conscious of her distinction of character as well as of mind. But partly as a result of her fine qualities, she was very slow to attribute evil motives to anyone or to detect methods that were repugnant to her own instincts. Nor was she naturally a good administrator, and I think she found much of her routine everyday work difficult. It was not her rôle to play a similar part to that of Miss Faithfull in the students' activities, and though her influence on some few was great and lasting, the majority never came close enough to understand and appreciate her great qualities. Nor could she fire their imagination or rouse their enthusiasm at a general meeting, whatever may have been the case with a small class of the philosophically minded.

In consequence there was a gradual but distinct deterioration in the corporate life of the College. Moreover, it appeared that there was a parallel decline in the competence to deal with the various committees of management. At any rate, certain fatal steps were taken without quick enough comprehension of where they would lead. Thus she was persuaded to allow the appeal for financial support to be made for the new Domestic Science venture alone, without reference to the rest of the Department, doubtless because this seemed most likely to produce good returns. The result was devastating, for when the money came in, it could be spent only on the object for which it had been contributed. The rest of the Department was in worse case than before; its liabilities were greater, since they included responsibility for the new venture, and there was now no prospect that it would be able to migrate to the buildings on Campden Hill when these were ready for occupation. In fact, they were designed and opened for the use of the Domestic Science Faculty only, and the rest of the Department remained in Kensington Square.

The next blow was the result of the Haldane Report on the future of the University of London, which was published in 1913. This recommended, among many other things, that owing to its lack of funds and adequate accommodation, the Women's Department of King's College should be amalgamated, as far as the Faculties of Arts and Science were concerned, with the parent body in the Strand. The classes for 'casual' students, the teaching of music and fine art were to come to an end, and only regular undergraduate students, now roughly about one hundred in number, were to migrate to King's College, with their Vice-Principal as Tutor to Women Students, and with certain of the more prominent women teachers as regular members of the staff in their respective subjects. The outbreak of war in August

1914 prevented the Haldane Report taking effect in any of its other suggestions and provisions, but this one recommendation had already been accepted by the University, in spite of protests from Kensington. In July 1914 the Women's Department came to an end as a separate institution, though it could not be completely merged with King's College for several years as it had first to pay off the debts incurred for the new institution in Campden Hill, henceforward to be known – the final straw – as King's College for Women (now King's College of Household and Social Science).

At this stage my own work at King's College ceased. I was offered a full-time appointment on its staff but was not prepared to accept the new conditions and to relinquish my work elsewhere. Thus my active connection with King's came to an end after twenty-two years as student and teacher – years which transformed and enriched my life in countless ways. My successor as lecturer in English at King's College was my former pupil and friend, the **HON. ELEANOR PLUMER**, now Principal of the St Anne's Society (Society of Home Students) in the University of Oxford.

CHAPTER 6:

Other interests

No-one active-minded could live and work in London during her formative years without becoming caught up in many and varied streams of interest. Certainly I did not confine myself to my professional work, though it, and the research which it involved or suggested, always had first claim, whatever else might call for attention. My interest in social conditions and political happenings was indeed at least in part the direct result of my study of literature. So, to some extent, was my interest in the theatre, as it was of course part of my business as a lecturer in English to study modern drama. Thus I was a constant spectator of the Elizabethan Stage Society[47] productions and, later, of the Phoenix Society[48] revivals of old plays. It was also my privilege to be a constant visitor to the Court Theatre[49] and to see most of the early performances of such of MR SHAW's plays as first appeared after I was grown up. Similarly, I was lucky enough to be present at the new productions of the plays of

47 The Elizabethan Stage Society was founded in 1894 by William Poel. His productions featured an Elizabethan-style stage, without scenery, and were played in halls and courtyards as well as theatres. He was a powerful influence on Shakespearean production in the first half of the twentieth century.

48 Founded by Montague Summers, the Phoenix Society ran from 1919 to 1925, over which period twenty-six influential productions were performed. The Society put on one restoration comedy each year, including works by Marlowe, Jonson and Beaumont and Fletcher.

49 A small theatre in Sloane Square, Chelsea. From 1904, it was managed for some years by Granville-Barker and put on many of Shaw's plays, and others by Ibsen, Galsworthy and Masefield *inter alia*. It later became the Royal Court.

Mr Masefield, including *Nan*, of Granville-Barker and of Galsworthy.[50]

Those Court Theatre productions were great fun, over and above the excitements of the plays themselves, because especially at Stage Society performances everybody who was anybody in the intellectual world was present, and one had the delightful sensation of hobnobbing with the great, even if they were unknown to me personally. Then there were the early English presentations of Ibsen's plays in William Archer's renderings and the tremendous repercussions of the Norwegian's influence on British drama as evidenced in the aforementioned dramatists in particular and, in another way, on Yeats, Lady Gregory, Synge and the Irish National Theatre. These plays provided very different fare from that of the commercial theatre of the day, of which the chief lights were Pinero and Henry Arthur Jones. But as the Bancrofts and Wyndham were still the main actors in comedy, even 'well-made' plays based on the fashion set by Sardou and Dumas fils were worth seeing, and Irving and Ellen Terry were actors who could make one forget the feebleness of the stuff they sometimes put across.

Nor must I omit the names of Eleonora Duse, Forbes-Robertson and Beerbohm Tree in even a cursory account of the theatre in my young days. I once enjoyed within a few weeks the remarkable treat of seeing Mrs Patrick Campbell, Sarah Bernhardt and Eleonora Duse successively take the

---

50   John Edward Masefield was Poet Laureate from 1930 until his death in 1967. He wrote poetry, novels and plays; *The Tragedy of Nan* (1908), directed by Harley Granville-Barker, ran successfully in England and America. Granville-Barker was an English actor, playwright and producer; he became co-manager of the Court Theatre and produced first performances of plays by Schnitzler, Hauptmann, Yeats, Galsworthy and Shaw. John Galsworthy, English novelist and playwright, is best known for *The Forsyte Saga* (1922), but also wrote a number of plays on social and moral themes.

name part in *La Dame aux Camélias* – an unforgettable experience. Many years later I saw Sarah Bernhardt play principal boy in a pantomime, but that was in Paris and after she had lost her leg. I was too young to be present at any of her performances when she was at her zenith, but I shall always remember the beauty of her voice and of her laugh. Of Duse, I was an ardent admirer and saw her in many rôles.

Finally, the Gilbert and Sullivan operas were appearing all through my girlhood and youth, and there is no question that by their art and satire these contributed very vitally to the rejuvenation of the theatre, as well as to the exposure of current follies and pretensions. Unfortunately, as I am almost absolutely tone deaf I cannot speak at first hand of most of even these, let alone of Covent Garden opera, Albert Hall or Queen's Hall concerts, or of such masters as Joachim, Ysaÿe, Kreisler, Caruso, Adelina Patti and Mme Melba, all of whom flourished in my youth.[51]

Often our visits to the theatre were to the pit or even the gallery, and that was in itself adventurous when one had been brought up to think that at least the dress circle and full evening dress were necessary accompaniments of such pleasures. As in my family expensive seats could be afforded only three or four times a year at most, I soon decided they were a quite unnecessary luxury and descended gradually to cheaper and more frequent visits to the theatre. In this I was following the fashion of my contemporaries, for many

---

51 Joseph Joachim was a Hungarian violinist and composer. The Belgian violinist, composer and conductor Eugène Ysaÿe was regarded as one of the most skilful performers of his time. Vienna-born Fritz Kreisler studied medicine but turned to the violin to become a successful virtuoso. Enrico Caruso was an Italian tenor regarded as one of the finest of all time. Dame Nellie Melba (real name Helen Porter Mitchell) was a highly successful Australian operatic soprano and pioneer recording artist, known for her numerous 'farewell' performances. The Italian soprano Adelina Patti was thought by Verdi to be the finest singer who ever lived.

middle-class women and girls were discovering – to begin with at matinées, later at the evening performances – that it was quite possible to enjoy a play when it was viewed from the pit, even when the seats were hard benches and not as luxurious as they are today. Nor did we meet with any of the rudeness of which we were warned by our elders.

Another discovery, productive of a good deal of innocent pleasure, was that of the cheap Italian and French restaurants in Soho where one could procure a reasonably good dinner before the theatre at a price within very limited means. I owed many a pleasant prelude to an evening's play-going to Petit-Riche[52] and some of his confrères. I well remember a notice on the wall of one such place – near Charing Cross, not in Soho – which proclaimed that 'Women are not allowed to smoke here. Ladies will not wish to do so.' I also remember being asked to leave an ABC[53] in Oxford Street because I insisted on finishing a cigarette. But these are digressions.

As I look back I seem to have been mixed up with a variety of learned and other societies. I was for some time on the Executive of the Modern Language Association, and quite soon after the end of my undergraduate days, Dr Furnivall insisted that I should become a member of the Philological Society and 'show my paces', i.e. read a paper there.

---

52 One of a number of small Soho restaurants at the time which offered economical versions of *haute cuisine*.

53 The Aerated Bread Company (ABC) was founded in 1862 and opened England's first public teashop in 1864; a chain of them followed. Tea shops were one of the first public places where it was permissible for a Victorian woman to eat a meal without a male escort, and without risking her reputation. Indeed the ABC tea shops were recommended to delegates of the Congress of the International Council of Women held in London in July, 1899. They were a significant feature of the period, frequently mentioned in literature, and provided an environment in which suffragettes and feminists generally were able to meet.

Dr Furnivall deserves more than a passing tribute from anyone who had the privilege of his acquaintance. I first met him at our College Browning Society where he came to hold forth on the poet and his writings. The next step followed in due course. He offered us the use of the boats at his Hammersmith Sculling Club so that we might have a College Boat Club of our own. These two things are typical of the man: his interests and his unfailing readiness to give pleasure and assistance, especially to the young and ignorant. He was, without exception, more generous of his time and knowledge than anyone of whom I have ever heard of comparable distinction, and with comparable calls upon his time. He was over seventy-five when I first made his acquaintance – a man with the heart and vigour of a boy. For another ten years he took his ABC girls – teashop waitresses – out on the river every Sunday and taught them to scull, and afterwards danced with them and their friends at the club house at Hammersmith which he had provided for them. Day after day he walked from Primrose Hill to the Reading Room at the British Museum to pursue his own studies or to look up references for correspondents, old and young, who had asked his help.

He had something of the impish mischief as well as of the liveliness and enthusiasm of a clever, devil-may-care boy, and was up to all sorts of tricks to the end of his days. But like a healthy boy in this also, he rejoiced in 'life, the mere living':[54] he found the world a good place, and he made it so for others by his own enjoyment and many-sided interests. He radiated fire and light. Founder of the Early English Text Society and the Chaucer, Shakespeare, Shelley and

---

54   A (mis)quotation from Robert Browning's *Saul* (1845): 'How good is man's life, the mere living! How fit to employ all the heart and the soul and the senses forever in joy!'

Browning Societies, he was instrumental in making early texts available in print, in revolutionising Shakespearian study and in popularising and spreading the knowledge of Browning's poetry. For half a century he was Secretary of the Philological Society, and to him more than to any other single individual are due the inception and carrying out of the plan for the great Oxford English Dictionary which originated from it.

Dr Furnivall was a keen scholar, ready – sometimes too ready – to accept and acclaim new theories and discoveries. For example, he unearthed an 'unknown' poem of Browning in an old Rugby School Magazine and had it reprinted and distributed among all his friends and acquaintances. Only then did he learn from the writer's mother that it was a schoolboy parody. I have my copy still, I am glad to say, but it was not safe to refer to it again in the presence of the donor. As for Manly's suggestions about the supposed authorship of Piers Plowman,[55] Furnivall joyfully received them at their face value long before the professional medievalists had a chance to examine them. To the very end of his life he retained his interest in every aspect of English scholarship, together with his lively sympathy and engagement with the various workers. Nor did he lay down his own tools until that last meeting of the Philological Society, which no-one then present can ever forget, when he summoned his friends to receive his resignation a very few weeks before his anticipated death. Characteristically he appeared to enjoy the announcement – which overwhelmed his listeners – for was not death itself only another adventure into the unknown?

Much could be related of his social experiments, his friendships with many and sundry in all walks of life, his

---

55 Manly had suggested that the three versions of Piers Plowman were by
     different authors. The debate continued for many years.

quarrels and practical jokes, and his ABC tea-parties in Tottenham Court Road; of his unconventional behaviour and clothes, and his correspondence – mostly conducted on picture postcards, often of a startling nature and in questionable taste. But I will refer to only one other of his peculiarities: his invariable use of women's Christian names when he was favourably inclined to their owners. Nowadays, when Christian names are in common use by both sexes, this would pass without notice or remark. In those days, when women used them among themselves only as a sign of great intimacy and men practically never, except among relatives, it was an innovation which must have been embarrassing to his women friends in the Doctor's younger days and was sufficiently startling even when he was nearing eighty.

Changed customs in this respect are worth a remark. In my undergraduate days, women – even students and colleagues – carefully 'miss-ed' each other in public unless they resorted to nicknames. Christian names were used only in private and then only between close friends. Men called each other only by their surnames, and little boys at prep schools forbade their parents to address envelopes with their Christian names in full lest these should become public property and result in ragging (see Benson's *David Blaize*,[56] where fun is made of this convention). I grew up among four brothers whose schoolfellows constantly visited at our home, but I do not remember ever to have known anything but their surnames, except in the case of the friends of my youngest brother, i.e. well on in the present century. I still recall the first time I heard two adults – they were Dr H.Y.C. Bradley and Mr Geo. Lyttleton – address each other publicly by their Christian names at a committee meeting of the English Association: it came as a kind of minor shock to my unaccustomed ears.

---

56 *David Blaize* (1916), set before World War I, describes the hero's school life in prep and public school.

Similarly, I have noted with interest the complete reversal of fashion that has since taken place in this respect, so that, for example, male undergraduates nowadays almost invariably use Christian names for each other and generally for their girl colleagues, while women commonly talk of and to each other by their surnames. In the same way, I still remember the first time I heard an adult refer to 'Daddy' – a name used only by very small children in my youth. In my own very early days we called our parents 'Mama' and 'Papa': later these terms were replaced by 'Mother' and 'Father'. 'Mum' and 'Dad' if used at all, were employed only by the ill-bred; 'Mummy' and 'Daddy' only by babies learning to talk.

The English Association, mentioned above, was another body in which I took – and take – an active interest. It was founded in 1906 as a means 'for intercourse and co-operation amongst all those interested in English Language and Literature' and to promote the study and teaching of English. I like to remember that I was present at the initial meetings and that I have been closely connected in one or another capacity with most of its undertakings, though usually in only a minor rôle.

But it is a pleasure to recall the association with such men as **DR A.C. BRADLEY**[*] under whose chairmanship I was privileged to serve on the selection committee which prepared *Poems of Today* (the second volume [1922]); that I was a member of the Executive Committee when it included, among others, such men as Sir Arthur Acland, Mr De la Mare, Sir

---

[*] Older folk who have had work published at Oxford will appreciate the following incident. When I congratulated Dr Bradley on his appointment to the Professorship of Poetry he said meditatively that at last he knew he had achieved greatness for the Clarendon Press now allowed him to spell judgment without an *e* and words ending in -ise with *s* and not *z* – privileges not permitted to lesser writers who must submit to the Oxford normalised spelling.

John Squire, Mr John Bailey and Sir E.K. Chambers;[57] that I have been and am associated with the *Year's Work in English Studies* and its tireless editor Dr Boas; that I have lectured to many of its branches and assisted in the formation of one of them; and that I have been permitted to write pamphlets for the Association, to contribute to *Essays and Studies* and to *English*, and even on one memorable and awe-inspiring occasion to propose the toast of the Association at the dinner when Lord Oxford and Asquith[58] officiated as its President. These are vainglorious memories but they also serve to emphasise my belief in the task which the English Association set out to perform, and which it has never ceased to endeavour to accomplish. By the measure of its success and not least by the part it played in the *Report of the Teaching of English in England* (1921), the Association has fully justified the hopes of its founders and proved its competence for renewed efforts in the future.

57 Arthur Acland was an English politician and social reformer with a strong interest in education. Walter De la Mare, a prolific English poet and author, wrote over 1000 poems and about 100 short stories. John Bailey was a writer on literature, and variously Chairman and President of the English Association. The theatre historian and civil servant E.K. Chambers was the author of *The Mediaeval Stage* (1903) and *The Elizabethan Stage* (1923); he also pursued a career in the Education Department and was involved in promoting adult education and the WEA. Sir John Squire was a British poet, writer, historian and an influential editor of the post-World War I period, working for the *London Mercury* and the *New Statesman*. Frederick Boas was a prolific scholar of early modern drama who was still writing when in his nineties. He was the first Honorary General Secretary, and later President, of the English Association.

58 Herbert Henry Asquith, 1st Earl of Oxford and Asquith, was Liberal MP for East Fife, Home Secretary 1892–5, Chancellor of the Exchequer 1905–8 and Prime Minister 1908–16.

CHAPTER 7:

Reading, college and university

One November day in 1901 I was looking forward to a First
XI hockey match in which I was to play as a substitute on the
following Saturday, when I received a mysterious and unexpected reply-paid telegram. It invited me to go to lunch on
that day with the 'Principal. College... Reading', to discuss a
possible appointment. I had never heard of the College and
to this day do not know how it had heard of me. I didn't particularly want any more work and I did desperately want to
play in that First XI match against Royal Holloway College.
So it took me an appreciable time to decide to accept the invitation and thus unwittingly to determine the whole course
of my future career.

When I arrived at the station no-one was able to direct
me to the College, so insignificant and unknown it still was
to the man in the street. Consequently I was late for lunch
and still remember the embarrassment I felt when shown
into a Common Room full of men and with no other woman
present. Of course it can't really have been the case, but my
memory is of being offered the cruet by everyone at table,
and at any rate that lasting impression indicates my state
of mind. One real occurrence remains. Lunch was nearly
over and many of the men had their unlit pipes in their
hands. I could not know that, owing to the small size of
the room, smoking was forbidden before 1.45, so I thought
they were politely waiting on my account. When therefore the Principal (now **SIR HALFORD MACKINDER**) offered
me a cigarette for the first time in my life in public among
strangers, out of sheer shyness I accepted and smoked it. To
this day I remember my indignation when on my next visit
to the College, I received a message from the authorities

requesting me to refrain from smoking in the Common Room.

At the interview which followed luncheon, I was asked if I would undertake to teach Anglo-Saxon to the first student of the College to require such instruction, since she was reading English for the London Intermediate (Honours) examination, and whether I would also prepare another girl for German BA Honours, and conduct an elementary German class for science students and some other beginners. My knowledge of colloquial German, after my three years of schooling in Hanover, was of course good, but neither at that time nor later was I ever qualified to undertake responsibility for work of a university standard in that subject. However I was assured that I should find myself equal to the task, and it still amuses me to remember that my first Honours student at Reading was in German, and that she ultimately obtained her degree in that subject; whether because of or in spite of my efforts I should not like to say.* In fact, I continued to teach German as well as English for many years, and I think it was not until 1913 that a full-time specialist was first appointed.

The remuneration offered me for one half day's work a week for the three terms was £30, to include railway fares.†

---

* As the lady in question has recently left a legacy to the University, it may be assumed that she did not feel she had been badly treated.

† The year before, first Miss Spurgeon and then I were offered some work at a Women's College which entailed spending one night weekly away from London. Each of us in turn refused the job because of the inadequacy of the payment proposed. The woman who was ultimately appointed was offered nearly double the sum we had rejected. We used to instance this as a proof that it was useful for women not absolutely dependent on their earnings to enter the labour market since only they could stand out against sweating. For it was in those days constantly necessary to justify a girl's desire for economic independence, which supposedly threatened the livelihoods of the unfortunates who were obliged to work – an argument never raised in reference to her brothers.

When I indignantly rejected these terms, they were at once doubled without discussion, and for £60 a year I accepted the work with the status of Assistant to the Vice-Principal W.M. Childs, at that time also lecturer in History and English Literature. On the following Thursday afternoon I went down to hold my first classes.

It will be gathered that the College was still in a very embryonic condition, and indeed it had come into being only in the session 1892/3, and its aims and future policy were still in the making. The full history of its beginnings and development may be read by those interested, in *Making a University* by W.M. Childs (Dent, 1933). Here I shall attempt nothing but an account from the personal standpoint of one whose life was closely bound up with its work and history in those early days, but who played no part in framing its policy, and merely an insignificant one in carrying it out. But like almost all who worked at the College in whatever capacity, I was soon infected by the spirit of enthusiasm and belief in its possibilities which permeated the atmosphere of the place and irradiated even routine work with the light of adventure.

The College had been founded at the suggestion of Christ Church, Oxford, which had offered the services of Mr Mackinder as its Principal. It was an outcome of the Reading University Extension Association, itself the result of the new Oxford University Extension movement of which the first centre was in Reading. When it was proposed to associate the classes held under its auspices with the technical instruction provided in Reading by the Department of Science and Art at South Kensington and with the training already given to pupil teachers in the evening and on Saturday, the idea was to 'blend the humane arts with scientific and technical instruction'. In the preface to the first Reading Calendar (1892/3), the object was defined as 'to bring education of a University type within the reach of those who cannot go to the University. Its function is to stimulate the desire for intellectual life, to diffuse both liberal and technical education, to train good citizens'.

When I first arrived upon the scene in the session 1901/2, the foundations had already been well and truly laid, and the University Extension College had recently been recognised as a Day Training College for elementary teachers. It had eighty full-time students who were preparing for the Teachers' Certificate, awarded after two years' study; these formed the majority of the full-time day students in humane and scientific subjects, but there were also a handful of students who were reading for external London degrees, and two or three of these had already been obtained. The Departments of Agriculture and Horticulture had been established and were stronger in numbers and finances than other parts of the institution; the School of Art and the School of Music were integral branches, and the former especially was already doing excellent work and attracting students in crafts as well as in fine art. Moreover, these heterogeneous elements were gradually blending into a whole which was conscious of its unity. But though much had been accomplished, much remained to be done before a true College could emerge from these elements. Above all, it was essential to develop those humane and scientific studies which are the necessary background to all technical applications of knowledge as well as the mainspring of education and of culture.

Mr Mackinder's tenure of the office of Principal was drawing to its close, and I personally experienced little of his influence and driving force which had set the wheels of progress in motion in the earlier years of the College. Mr Childs had become Vice-Principal when I first arrived in 1900 and it was already he who was the mainspring and fount of energy of the whole place. The town was small and not particularly interested, even if not actively opposed to the foundation of a college in its midst; the available buildings were confined and inadequate to their purpose; the teaching staff was mainly non-resident and part-time; and most of the students were ill-prepared and not intellectually distinguished.

There appeared little to justify Mr Childs in his unswerving faith in the possibilities and future of the institution he was called upon less to direct than to create. Whatever is of value and peculiar to itself in the University of Reading is due, more than to any other cause or individual, to his vision and belief in the team spirit and in the quality of the education which is derived from work and play and life in common. It would be easy to point out weaknesses in his methods and achievements, very easy to criticise particular mistakes and errors of judgment as they appeared to me or to others. But the great fact remains in the accomplishment of what in those early days seemed impossible and was not envisaged at that time even by himself: the emergence of what is now the University of Reading as a living and vitalising force in British education.

Perhaps the description of just a few typical steps will best illustrate how progress was initiated. If the College was to become a society of like-minded individuals with common aims and aspirations, they must be united into a body which was conscious of its identity – this must apply to staff as well as students. One of the earliest steps taken in 1897 was the opening of a small Senior Common Room where meals could be served daily and occasional formal dinner parties instituted. This beginning developed when the College transferred to the present site into a staff club, which was for many years unique among the newer university institutions. By great good fortune there stood in the grounds – which ultimately came into the possession of the College – the house which had been the childhood home of the Palmer family,[59] the members of which were, together with **LADY WANTAGE**, the most generous and influential of the supporters of the new venture. **ALFRED PALMER**, who first leased and then presented the magnificent site on which the University stands,[60] expressed the wish that the old family home should be preserved. What he and his brother, the **RT. HON. GEORGE WILLIAM PALMER**, desired in such a matter obviously was binding, and thus there came into the possession of the Council a building not suitable for ordinary academic purposes, but most admirably adapted to those of the staff. An excellent and most attractive Senior Common Room could at once be established, opening on to delightful lawns which were reserved for the use of its members. A few years later, when the University Library was built – also by the munificence of the Palmer family and as a memorial to their brother George William – the upper rooms of the house until then used to house the library were transformed into a spacious staff dining room capable of accommodating as many as 150 persons, and in daily use for luncheon by anything from thirty to sixty people.

It would be difficult to exaggerate the beneficent influence of these common room club facilities on the communal life. At lunch, or at tea in the sitting room, at any hour convenient to themselves, outside on the bowling-green and in the garden, members of all faculties and departments, of both

---

59 The Palmer home was The Acacias, for many years the Senior Common Room of the University.

60 The London Road site.

sexes[*] and every status meet together, cement friendships, thrash out problems, argue, discuss and hear each other's point of view. One result is that at no period has there ever developed at Reading the departmental rivalry and exclusiveness that sometimes mar academic life. Another is the complete absence of any line of social demarcation between senior and junior members of staff. In Common Room the title of Professor is not used, and from the Vice-Chancellor to the most recently appointed Assistant, everyone meets his colleagues naturally and on equal terms.

Lay members of Council frequently profit by their right to become members of Common Room, to the benefit of all concerned. Private parties may be held in Small Common Room where it is also customary to entertain candidates for official positions before the formal appointing interviews are held; guests may be introduced to the ordinary meals, and these vary from official visitors of every kind to personal acquaintances of members. Each autumn term new members of staff are welcomed and entertained by their colleagues; when old friends depart they are given a send-off dinner. A treasured sign of regard at resignation is the rarely granted election to honorary membership of Common

---

[*] When we first moved to the new site the suggestion was made that what is now known as Small Common Room should be reserved for women. There were at that time only seven women on the academic staff, of whom I was the only one concerned with an ordinary university subject, the others being wardens of hostels (as they were then called) and teachers of Music and Fine Art. As every member of staff has and already had a private room for interviews and retirement when desired, we determined in no circumstances to avail ourselves of a separate women's common room and thus to risk gradual exclusion from intercourse with our male colleagues. The plan therefore did not mature, and there has never been a serious revival of the idea of segregation of the sexes, nor indeed was this contemplated when the suggestion of a women's common room was mooted.

Room, and, in brief, the club-like fellowship it provides becomes for most senior members of the University one of the outstanding and most appreciated features of its communal life. It is also one which invariably receives favourable comment from visitors from other universities, by no means all of which possess similar amenities even nowadays.

But I have passed on too rapidly to the present and must return to earlier days. If it was not easy to attain unity among a scattered and in the main part-time body of teachers, still less was it a simple matter to secure anything approaching a sense of common aims and interests among the student body, consisting as it did of most diverse elements. How to unite into a College with a corporate life of its own the worthy, middle-aged seekers after culture who attended University Extension lectures, the evening class students, mostly very youthful, who wished for instruction in technical subjects, the students of art and music, of agriculture and horticulture, the handful of degree students in arts and science, the teachers in training and the pupil teachers?

A good deal had been achieved before I first knew the College, much of it by means of the usual athletic clubs, debating society and the like. Certainly by the end of 1901 a newcomer was not predominantly conscious of the absence of corporate spirit, especially when her work lay wholly among the more serious, full-time students who already proudly sported academic dress. But quite soon I began to hear about something called the Gild of the Red Rose, and at Christmas 1902 (by that time promoted to the status of assistant lecturer) I was persuaded to attend its annual festival, or Jantaculum.

Now this Gild was something which differed from the usual academic society in that it was deliberately designed by Mr Childs as a partial means of overcoming the lack of cohesion he deplored as a hindrance to healthy development. The students' unions were still in their infancy and did not attract the most representative men and women; there were two small, privately-run residential hostels for women, but the bulk of the students who did not live at home resided in cheap lodgings where they enjoyed none of the amenities of a corporate organisation. In College there were most inadequate common rooms, there was no students' buttery, the newly acquired Athletic Ground was far away at the other end of the town and, though the river was close by, there were no College boats, let alone a boathouse. The Gild of the Red Rose was the first serious attempt to found a society which should gather together and attract all the members of the nascent College, whatever their special interest, staff and students alike, and unite them on common ground. It must appeal to the imagination by its ceremonial; it must inspire enthusiasm by its doings, both serious and trivial.

The young institution had no roots in the past, but at that time it was housed on the site of the most famous mediaeval abbey in southern England and in a town the history of which had been continuous and important for many centuries. The historic sense was aroused by the adaptation of the phraseology, vows and rules of the ancient Gild Merchant of Reading,[61] which were taken over with little modification. The officers and members addressed each other as Curiani and Gildani; their meetings were called Morowspeches or Gemots; their festivals were Jantacula, their tea-parties or

61 A powerful association of merchants within the town, consisting of between 20 and 50 burgesses from various trades. Eventually it assumed responsibility for local government in Reading. New entrants had to provide a Jantaculum, or feast.

suppers Gild Meles. The Curia bedecked themselves in red robes on state occasions; the members all sported red roses or rosettes; the Gild had its banner and its song; it became the emblem and sign of College unity.

The mummery may have been childish but it was taken very seriously by young and by old, and it led them gently towards the paths of more serious study. The weekly Morowspeches, always preceded by a Gild Mele (tea) presided over by the Gustator, were devoted to the reading aloud by the members of literature of all kinds – plays, poetry, essays, fiction, modern and ancient, serious and humorous. There was no limit to the range except that of excellence of quality. 'Fine literature' was read 'for the sake of the fine pleasure which it affords'. The Gild tried to spread the realisation of that pleasure among all and sundry, not by talking about it but by enjoying the experience. The hundreds of young folk who flocked week by week to these Gild meetings needed no exhortations to make them realise that the heritage of English literature belongs to all and is not the possession merely of the specialist. The communal experience gave them the opportunity to enter in and enjoy, and it also created a strong bond of union between the participants. The Gild stood for recreation, the re-creation derived from wholesome enjoyment; and that to be derived from fine literature became palpable to many who would not have discovered it for themselves in isolation from the good fellowship which went along with it.

In addition to the ordinary Morowspeches and the less frequent and small Gemots which attempted more solid reading, the Gild held at least once a year a Jantaculum. This was a public entertainment of a unique kind, a variety show of a high standard which included acting, music, dancing and song, but which had nothing in common with commercial performances. Often the libretto was specially written and centred on some historical event or subject; sometimes a period was illustrated by every type of its artistic production; or an author, for example Dickens, might provide the staple of the subject matter. On occasion, but not in its most characteristic ventures, a mediaeval or sixteenth- or seventeenth-century play was selected as the centrepiece. As often and as far as was possible every Gild member present was dressed in the costume of the selected period. Very often proceedings started with a procession round the hall, or the actual items occurred as interruptions to the perambulations of the general company which halted and made a circle round the actors or dancers as they played their parts. Or the waits [carol singers, Ed.] mingled with the crowd which joined in the carols, or a sedan chair provided rides for any who were willing to entrust themselves to the bearers.

Always in the earlier winter Jantacula, the supper was a sit-down Christmas meal, followed by speeches from the Custos, Reeve and Public Orators, and by the solemn parade of the Christmas Pudding accompanied by an adaptation of the Magdalen boar's head song.

> Plum-pudding in hand bear we
> Bedecked with bay and rosemary
> We pray you, Gildani, be merry
> Qui estis in Jantaculo.

It is difficult to convey the aroma and spirit of these celebrations, but it is certain that their renown spread far beyond Reading. The important thing to notice here is that the Gild did more than any other single agency to help College life and to promote College unity. It was not for nothing that Gildani vowed solemnly at their initiation 'to labour always for the common weal, the increase of humane learning, the honour of this College and the fair name of our Gild'.

Some people thought in those days that there was too much talk about unity, about a college being a society and not merely a seat of learning, and about the 'life' of the student body. Looking back nowadays, one can see how the insistence on this theme ministered to the right development of the academic society and helped it to grow and prosper. It is certain that the young institution managed from the beginning to avoid some of the weaknesses often found in the newer British universities and colleges, and most of his colleagues would agree that this was largely owing to the Principal's conception of what should come first in the building-up of a centre of liberal education. Quite briefly, it must be a meeting place for those who seek as teachers and as learners to make themselves useful members of society and to promote its welfare by mutual education. It must be the nursery of those fitted to serve society 'in Church and State' according to the formula of the old University Bidding Prayer – a place where mind clashes with mind, and knowledge with knowledge; where truth is sought and where, amid a variety of occupations and interests, tolerance is learned, friendships are formed and young people are trained to independence and citizenship.

There is nothing new in this conception which goes back to the mediaeval theory of the 'universitas' – according to Rashdall[62] the term originally applied to the 'scholastic body', not to 'the place in which such a body was established or even its collective Schools'. University does not and never did imply a school of universal learning. 'Universitas' referred to the community, not to its studies. The building of a community is, then, historically, the recognised first step in the evolution of an academic institution. In this view Childs

---

62 Hastings Rashdall, a historian and theologian, was the author of *Universities of Europe in the Middle Ages* (1895) and many religious works.

never wavered, and his influence secured development upon those lines and served to shape and direct policy.

For example, in 1905, after apparently never-to-be-ended efforts, an adequate site was secured upon which there was space for necessary buildings both immediately and in the future. The administrative offices and the Letters subjects migrated to their present quarters forthwith. They were, and for the most part still are, inadequately accommodated in a terrace of converted Georgian houses which form part of the frontage of the ten acres upon which there was room to build and extend in every direction. There was obvious and immediate need to construct laboratories and studios so that the various departments could be reunited. Money was, as always, very short, and it was necessary to balance conflicting claims. To many, it was an unexpected decision to begin with a Great Hall which could become a central meeting place for the whole College. There were many criticisms from disgruntled teachers in cramped and unsuitable quarters, but there can be little doubt that the plan of campaign adopted showed strategic wisdom.

On 7th October 1908, Lady Wantage presided at the inaugural dinner of the Hall for men students which bears her name and of which she was the munificent and sympathetic founder. Wantage Hall was the first attempt to secure for our men the benefits of corporate residence and the advantages derived from the mutual education, the loyalties, ideals and traditions which develop as the result of a life lived in common. With its foundation, a seal was set upon the residential policy which has characterised and distinguished Reading among the British provincial Universities and, in the words of the official letter announcing the fact, it was ultimately 'mainly owing to the well-developed residential system established by the College' that, in spite of its limitations in respect of income and of numbers, a University

Charter was granted. From the day when Wantage Hall was opened, all full-time day students not residing with their parents or guardians have been required to live in a University Hall, of which there are now two for men and three for women.

The policy which was in part forced upon us because the town of Reading was not of sufficient size to supply more than a small proportion of the students was nevertheless chiefly due to the wisdom and foresight of those who directed its fortunes. In the recently published *Red Brick University*, the author[63] contrasts, very much to their disadvantage, the contribution commonly made by the new provincial universities to the physical and moral welfare of their undergraduate members, compared with the amenities offered by Oxford and Cambridge. In so far as men and women live at home this is to some extent unavoidable, especially in great cities where distances entail long daily journeys. But that this has not always been the sole determining factor is proved by the general provision nowadays of residential accommodation for students of both sexes who would without it be relegated to life in lodgings.

Reading has also been the pioneer among newer universities[*] in its imitation of the Oxford tutorial system. From very early days, every regular student has been assigned to a tutor who is responsible not merely for the supervision of

63 Bruce Truscott (real name E. Allison Peers), *Red Brick University* (1943). The book was influential and controversial and argued in favour of the primacy of research over teaching in universities.

* Compare what was said about King's College, Women's Department, on p.79/80. It was a remarkable coincidence, and for me very fortunate, that the tutorial system was introduced in both the institutions where I worked.

his work and timetable but also for his general welfare. It is almost impossible to exaggerate the importance of this personal relationship between teachers and taught; and while I can speak with certainty and detailed knowledge only of my own Faculty, I know that no student of humane letters at Reading has ever had cause to complain of any barrier to intercourse between dons and undergraduates. Nor have I reason to suppose that the same thing is not true of all parts of the University. My experience confirms my belief in the merit of this relationship, which often results in lasting friendships. To this day I am in regular correspondence with many former pupils of both sexes, some of whom are already grandparents, and I know I am not singular in this respect. Old Students' Reunions constantly testify to the durability of such associations, the value of which is not by any means one-sided.

I have mentioned the site for the central University buildings which came into our possession in 1905 through the munificence of Mr Alfred Palmer. These extensive and beautifully laid out grounds have ministered notably to the well-being of the institution. It is of course of primary importance to have space to breathe and opportunity for expansion. But our lines had also fallen in pleasant places. There was room and to spare: there were magnificent trees of many varieties, there were flowers and birds. No need here to erect a many-storeyed lofty building in imitation Gothic or Georgian style. No need either to build for today without leaving room for future growth and expansion. The two main considerations were first to preserve as much of the beauty and as many of the trees as might be; secondly to evolve a plan which should be as little costly as possible and yet combine convenience and seemliness with as much of dignity as could be achieved with the means available.

It was finally decided to erect a series of low workshop style buildings separated by gardens and opening on to cloisters enclosing a spacious quadrangle. At the north end of the cloisters there were ultimately grouped the University Library, connected by another cloister with the Great Hall and the War Memorial Clock Tower. This layout necessitated considerable walking about from one block to the other, but it has inestimable advantages in the preservation of trees, open spaces and natural beauty. Every window in the Library opens on to a green vista; every Department is separated from the next by its garden. There is room to saunter and to converse, and this compensates for the absence of any dignified entrance from the front. Indeed the modest gateway between ordinary-looking houses may easily be overlooked by the would-be visitor, nor does the long tunnel-like passage with the porter's box on one side convey any impression of entrance to academic precincts. The effect is more reminiscent of an underground railway station!

But if external dignity has hitherto been sacrificed, most people will agree that as far as means permitted, the best possible use has been made of the grounds themselves. Much remains to be done. There is still no Students' Union House, there are no Small Hall, no Council or Senate rooms, no adequate home for St David's Hall (the hall for non-resident students), and no common room accommodation for the secretarial and office staff. But at any rate nothing needs to be undone and the charm and attraction of the simple layout speak for themselves and make their appeal alike to visitors and to members of the University. The same thing applies to the exceptionally beautiful playing fields which are within ten minutes' walk of the central site, and to the gardens attached to the various Halls of Residence, more particularly those for women. And nowadays there are two admirable boathouses side by side on the Thames, and a gymnasium in the main grounds.

All these material benefits are the outcome of and minister to that corporate spirit of which we used to hear so much in the early days. Now there is no need to talk of it, for no man or woman works at Reading University in any capacity without coming under its all-pervasive influence. Traditions necessarily grow up slowly in a new institution, but half a century has sufficed firmly to establish at Reading the tradition of comradeship in a common cause. Upon this it will be possible, with time and opportunity, to build up an academic society of permanent and far-reaching importance, even though it may remain small in numbers and without the full complement of Faculties.

In this connection one other Reading practice worthy of note also originated in the conception of its first Vice-Chancellor. From very early days, Childs realised the mutual advantages to be derived from close collaboration between lay and academic members of the governing bodies. Little by little the custom was established that representatives of both sections of the community should meet on all types of committee and thrash out their problems together. On Selection Committees, Halls of Residence Committees, on the Research Board, among the Curators of the Library, on the Military Education Committee and the rest, the Council[64] are fully represented, while on the Council, in addition to the Vice-Chancellor and the Deans of Faculties (three), there sit two representatives of the Senate and one from each Faculty Board (three in all). On the Finance Committee, which consists of thirteen members in all, with the Registrar as secretary, there are four members of the Senate in addition to the Vice-Chancellor.

---

64 Council is the governing body of the University; members include representatives of all areas of the University, plus 15 non-University members.

There is no doubt that this co-operation results in understanding of conflicting views, toleration of differences and general smoothness of working in many directions. It also ensures that lay members of Council get first-hand acquaintance with many aspects of University life of which they might otherwise know little or nothing.[*]

It is time to retrace our steps from the present and return to the formative years when the foundations were being laid. It was at the beginning of the session 1902–3 that the name University College was adopted to mark its first receipt of a grant from the Treasury Commissioners. True – the grant amounted only to £1000 a year and was conditional on a similar sum being raised locally for teaching of a university type in arts and science; but at that period only twelve other institutions in all obtained such Treasury grants, and the recognition of status was almost, if not quite, as valuable as the actual money. Moreover, favourable comment was made by the Commissioners on the 'enthusiasm' which was said to characterise the College and which was ascribed at any rate in part to the youthfulness of its teaching staff.

At the end of that session, Mr Mackinder resigned his office of Principal and Mr Childs was appointed his successor. At the same time I was promoted to be lecturer in English in his place, and from October 1903 until October 1912 I was solely responsible for the organisation and for almost all the teaching of the subject. Combined with my Lectureship at King's and the necessary travelling involved, I had plenty to

---

[*] The author of *Red Brick University* refers to the difficulties and delays which often occur at provincial universities in regard to new appointments. Perhaps it is due to the harmonious relations between the lay members of the Council and the academic staff that Reading is blissfully immune from these.

do, but the work was congenial and I thoroughly enjoyed it and also the atmosphere of keen endeavour and progressive energy which characterised both institutions. However, the unbroken pleasure in my work was doomed to unforeseen disturbance.

After the end of the summer term of 1907, at a special interview for the purpose, I was informed for the first time of the intention to reorganise the constitution of the College at Reading on university lines. Deans of Faculty were to be nominated, the heads of Departments were to be given the title of Professor, and Faculty Boards were to be established. From what was said I at first understood that the title of Professor was to be conferred only on some outstanding colleagues and it did not strike me as remarkable that I was not among the proposed recipients until, just as the discussion was terminating, I discovered from the embarrassed reply to a casual question of my own that I was the sole lecturer in charge of a subject who was to be omitted from the list.

I still think that I should have submitted to the decision had I been told, what I believe to have been the fact, that a young and struggling institution with its reputation still in the making was afraid it might suffer if it risked being the first in the British Isles to give to a woman the title of Professor. An appeal of this nature to my loyalty might have prevailed, for I cared intensely for the welfare of the College and had no illusions about my own merits. I was a successful lecturer and teacher; I possessed the makings of a tolerable scholar and I was already engaged upon research work of importance. But I knew that I had no claim to outstanding intellectual gifts and that it was beyond my power to produce original work of a high order. Moreover it had not entered my head that I should ever attain the professorial status to which no woman in this country had hitherto been admitted.

Be that as it may, the appeal was not made and the whole business was conducted with considerable lack of tact and straightforwardness. It was specifically denied that the omission of myself from the list of professors-designate was due to my sex, my youth, my lack of distinction or to any other cause that could be named. This being so, I felt compelled to fight the decision, especially as there were some included in the new professoriate whose claims were considerably lower than my own, whether as scholars or teachers. I offered my resignation but was persuaded to withdraw it and to give the new arrangement a trial. After a session of petty pin-pricks and discomfort, some of them doubtless due to my over-sensitiveness on the subject, I refused to remain unless I were granted the title of Professor as from October 1908 – a year later than the institution of the rank at Reading. I was therefore at last nominated Professor, but of English Language, i.e. of the branch of my subject in which I was not and had no intention of becoming a specialist, and I had to accept this compromise and also to agree to the intended subsequent institution of a Professorship of English Literature, though I was led to suppose that this would be in the nature of an Oxford Professorship of Poetry, and that I should remain in charge of the ordinary, day-by-day organisation and work of the Department on the literary as well as on the linguistic side.

The new appointment was not actually made until 1912, and when it came these suggestions were forgotten and my responsibility for English Literature, though not my teaching of it, came to an end. Nor were things made easier for me by the fact that the authorities did not trust me to keep to my bargain and to accept the changed position to which, however unwillingly, I had agreed. I may say at once that things would have been impossible from my point of view but for the absolute loyalty and understanding of my new colleague, Professor Dewar, who did everything in his power to make it tolerable. If conditions were very hard for me, they were certainly not easy for him, and I can but hope he found me equally anxious to make them workable for us both.

One incidental disadvantage in the new arrangement must be mentioned. In our small institution English became the sole subject which boasted two Professors, with the inevitable extra expense that this entailed. It was therefore obvious that in view of the prevalent lack of means, the arrangement could not be permanent and must cease when the time came for my retirement. Thus I have always been painfully conscious that my chair would be abolished when I reached the statutory age, and I have always worked with the unpleasant conviction that the necessary cost must outweigh the value of any service I could render the place whose interests I had at heart. It was a galling and unhappy result of my insistence on my position and one which I could never forget.

In fact the expected happened: I was superannuated (owing to the date of my birthday) within a few weeks of attaining my sixty-fifth year; the chair of English Language was abolished and a young lecturer was appointed at less than half my salary to carry on my work. Combined with the fact that my retirement fell at Michaelmas 1940, at the worst moment of the war, this did not make it any easier for me to sever my active connection with the University, though everything possible was done by colleagues and students to make the break as little painful as might be. Yet the overwhelming impression remains: 'We are hence, we are gone, as though we had not been there' [A.C. Swinburne, *A Leave-Taking*].

I have always regarded the long struggle for my position and title as my contribution to the battle for fair dealing for women in public and professional life. Certainly it gave me little personal satisfaction and was the cause of endless friction, important and unimportant. Here are two very dissimilar examples of difficulties not in my power to avoid. The first is trivial, but significant as a symbol of the general position: for months after its conferment some of the College clerks, probably with the connivance of their superior officer, persistently refused to use the title on official communications sent to me, until I was forced most reluctantly to take notice of the omission. The second trouble was much more serious. It was obvious that I needed assistance in the increasing work, and equally obvious that, in a co-educational establishment, since I was a woman, my lecturer ought to be of the other sex. But – so it was stated by the authorities – no man could be asked to serve under a woman. So when a very suitable candidate had been interviewed and offered part-time work, I was informed to my horror that it was proposed to appoint him under the Dean of the Faculty through whom I could transmit any suggestions or criticisms I might wish to make to the young lecturer, just down from Oxford – and this in spite of the fact that I ranked as responsible head of the English Department. I have no idea what the young man's reactions were to this amazing proposal, nor even if it was ever made to him. All I know is that I turned it down as unworkable. Before any way had been found out of this impasse, he was offered a much better post elsewhere and withdrew his application. When I returned to work after the Long Vacation no further steps had been taken and I was informed that I might myself secure assistance from any suitable woman known to me.

This arrangement persisted until 1911, when a full-time male lecturer was appointed and informed – it is only fair to say not by the Principal – that, as an English Literature chair would be instituted in the following year, he would not long be in the ignominious position of subordinate to a woman only. This man, who soon became an intimate friend, has often told me that this remark, coupled with other things said about his future attitude to me, very nearly caused his refusal of the post. In fact, as it turned out, the appointment was a complete success from every point of view, and the College was most lucky in retaining his services until his appointment to the Professorship of English at Bristol in 1920.

I have already said that I was the first woman to obtain the title of Professor at a British university or university college. In the circumstances it may justly be inferred that this was no cause of personal gratification or pride. But that it was of service to the position of university women is a fair assumption. The first step had been taken, and it was not long before the example was followed elsewhere. In the reorganised teaching University of London, it was comparatively natural and easy to appoint women to university professorships at Bedford College for Women, Royal Holloway College and the London School of Medicine for Women.

Then at various provincial universities some of the smaller and less important chairs, e.g. of Italian, were filled in the same way. Later on, King's and Birkbeck Colleges, the first educational colleges to do so in the University of London, appointed women professors respectively in Zoology (**PROFESSOR DORIS MACKINNON**) and Botany (Dame Helen Gwynne Vaughan): next Dr Helen Wodehouse became Professor of Education at Bristol, Dr Olive Wheeler filled the equivalent chair at Cardiff and, most significant of all, **DR POPE** was invited by Manchester to accept the chair of French. These were among the early examples of women professors in co-educational institutions: today there are also others. It is still the case that a woman stands no chance of appointment to a professorship unless she is head and shoulders above the available male competitors, but at any rate there is no longer an absolute or acknowledged sex bar.* Nor did it appear to excite any adverse comment when for the first time women professors were recently elected at both Oxford and Cambridge.†

Meanwhile my own status, though established, did not in practice put me on full equality with my colleagues, at any rate for many years. Not only was there never any suggestion that I should serve as an elected member of Council, but I was also seldom appointed to sit on any of the more important University committees, and when I could not be left out, I was seldom allowed to pull my full weight. However my professorial standing secured my unquestioned place on the Senate and Faculty Board when Reading obtained its University Charter. It also entitled me to take part in all the discussions and debates about the form and details of the Charter, Statutes, Ordinances and degree courses. Unfortunately for myself, I was unable to strengthen my position by the obvious means of voting in favour of the policy

---

* Should it be reckoned an advantage or a disadvantage that women are much less often invited than men to act as external examiners at other universities – a privilege and plague to which male professors are constantly subject? The advantages of such examinerships are experience of other universities and their standards as well as considerable additions to income. The disadvantage is the galling and soul-destroying duty of setting and correcting endless papers. In the course of my long career, I served for one period as External Examiner at the University of London. I have never been asked to serve elsewhere and I understand from my friends that a number of others among the older women professors are in the same case. An outstanding and very popular scientist, for example, told me she had never examined except in her own university. However, nowadays many exceptions could be cited, and these grow yearly more frequent.

† Other noticeable university appointments held by women are that of Registrar to the University of Bristol (Miss Shapland) and Librarian to the University of Reading (Miss Kirkus).

of the authorities, with which I did not agree. My opposition was due to an honest difference of opinion, but it confirmed the belief that I was either out to make trouble or simply unintelligent and unprogressive – possibly both.

For, as seems inevitable in all institutions at such times of crisis, we suffered badly from growing pains in the form of internal dissension during the period when we were striving to obtain University independence. There is no reason now to stir up the ashes of long extinguished fires. The First World War intervened, and, when it was over, our debates were resumed more amicably. Nor have there ever since been any disputes and disturbances at all comparable with those battles-royal about the proposed University constitution. The draft Charter, when submitted for acceptance, represented the agreed views of all the senior members of the academic staff and did not contain the proposed innovations in government against which some of us had felt obliged to protest.

For the greater part of the war period and for some time afterwards, I was again working single-handed in the English Department, with part-time help from my friend Miss Lee. There were no men students left in the Faculty of Letters during the latter years of the war, and only a handful of the physically unfit anywhere in the College. But there were more women than ever, since Mr Fisher had made a special appeal to them to complete their courses and prepare themselves for teaching as the most important war work they could undertake. Women lecturers were also asked to remain at their posts rather than to join the women's auxiliary forces or to become temporary civil servants. So there was no diminution in the type or number of lectures or classes or in the papers to be corrected, though, speaking for myself, there was often very great temptation to go off and take up a different job more obviously connected with the war effort.

On one occasion I nearly succumbed, when I was approached concerning an important position at one of the Ministries. There had just been more trouble about my temporary status while responsible for both branches of my subject during the absence of my colleagues in the army, and I therefore asked Mr Childs if he would prefer me to follow their example and apply for leave of absence for the period of the war. He made it plain that he did not feel able to fill my place and that it was his wish that I should remain at Reading. This settled the matter, and I am glad to say that from that moment – though my personal difficulties with one unreconcilable antagonist who took every opportunity, public and private, to humiliate me, did not end until his retirement many years later – there was no further trouble between Mr Childs and myself.

It is true that I was not nominally a full-time member of staff until 1920 – and then chiefly as the result of Professor Dewar's representations. But this and other matters of dispute did not originate with Mr Childs and, insofar as he was responsible, it was because he was too easily influenced by a more dominating personality. Mr Childs had some of the weaknesses as well as the strength of a highly imaginative mind. He had the artist's sensitiveness and desire for recognition as well as the artist's enjoyment in creation and translating his visions into reality. It is not an exaggeration to say he gradually became obsessed by his ideal university[*] and that he lived with the single-minded purpose of realising his conception. As this gradually shaped itself, he became more and more inclined to think that any form of criticism, unless from a trusted intimate, must arise from mere ignorance

---

[*] An irreverent young colleague was once heard to remark that if Childs had been marooned on a desert island, in ten years he would have got a university going.

or from a desire to thwart him. Moreover he was constitutionally unwilling to face public opposition and fearful lest it might injure his cause. Consequently he became increasingly influenced by those upon whose judgment he relied because he was certain of their support in his main schemes. This led in many cases to quite unnecessary doubts and difficulties for himself, and sometimes to apparent weakness in action.

On the other hand, as I have endeavoured to show, it was almost entirely due to his wisdom, enthusiasm and vision that the University of Reading came into being; that it was created in spite of almost every conceivable difficulty of position, lack of public demand and support; and that the foundations were laid in the right way and with certain modifications of the usual design which afforded a basis for strength and development. He accomplished admirably a self-imposed task and did so in such a way that the child of his conception will bear permanently the features he impressed upon it.

To the surprise of many, the name of Mr Childs appeared in no honours list, nor did the Borough of Reading confer its freedom upon him in acknowledgment of the fresh reputation the town was acquiring through his work. But the universities of Liverpool, Oxford and Reading in turn recognised his services to education by the conferment of an honorary doctorate, and there can be no question that he earned the right to rank among the foremost educationists of his day, and that this was recognised by all who were most competent to judge.

The Charter gained, Dr Childs became the first Vice-Chancellor of the new University and remained to guide it through the early formative years. He resigned at Michaelmas 1929, after thirty-six years of untiring and devoted service which had been crowned by the successful creation of a residential University at which men and women of small means could enjoy similar opportunities of comradeship and mutual education to those previously confined almost entirely to undergraduates at Oxford and Cambridge. Dr Childs was succeeded in the Vice-Chancellorship by DR (now Sir Franklin) SIBLY, at that date Principal of the University of London, who had previously served as Vice-Chancellor both of the University of Wales and of the University of Durham. Sir Franklin's wide experience of many institutions made him particularly valuable in a place which had so far been somewhat too self-contained and therefore 'insular' in outlook. He also possesses qualities which are ideally complementary to those of his predecessor. I think he would be the first to admit that he could not have created a new university, but no-one could work with him without speedily discovering his administrative and business ability, grasp of affairs, skill in judging character, impartiality and absolute fairness and readiness to hear everyone's point of view. Combined with strength of will and great personal charm, these things make for lack of friction and easy intercourse. While he gets his own way when he thinks it necessary to do so, he does it without creating any sense of grievance in his opponents, who feel that their opinion has been heard and carefully considered even though it may not have prevailed. It should be added that Sir Franklin and Lady Sibly have added strength to the University by the great popularity and influence they have acquired in the town.[*]

From the beginning it had been prominent in the minds of the founders of the University Extension movement and

---

[*] To the sorrow of his colleagues, Sir Franklin's resignation on the ground of ill health was regretfully accepted by the Council in June 1946. His wise counsel and genial personality will be sorely missed.

subsequently of the University Extension College, Reading, as far as possible to bring to those who could not go to a university some of the benefits of university education. Of this aim the College never lost sight in its day-by-day work. In addition to this it endeavoured to serve the town by means of very varied courses of public lectures which continued to make a systematic appeal to the type of audience – mainly middle-class, black-coated workers of every kind and their wives and daughters – for which the University Extension movement originally catered. In 1903 the inspiration of **DR ALBERT MANSBRIDGE** inaugurated a fresh adventure which was to have even more far-reaching effects. A meeting in Oxford saw the foundation of what afterwards became the Workers' Educational Association [WEA]. In the following year, largely owing to the enthusiastic co-operation of Mr Childs, the first local branch of the Association came into being at Reading.

My readers are probably aware that the WEA functions in its most advanced work through the co-operation of Joint Committees consisting of representative working men and women elected by themselves – nowadays from among members of the WEA – and of members of the nearest university or university college. These Joint Committees are responsible for the provision of such Tutorial Classes as are desired by not more than twenty-four members of the WEA who undertake to attend them. Each class meets twenty-four times a session for three successive years: each student undertakes, unless unavoidably prevented, to attend the whole course regularly and to do such written and other work as may be prescribed.

Tutor and class discuss and, as far as may be, arrange the syllabus and subjects of study together; the tutor usually lectures or talks for the first hour at each meeting of the class: the students spend the following hour with him in discussion and debate about the subject of the lecture. A class secretary, elected by the students, voluntarily undertakes responsibility for the regularity of their attendance and written work, collection of fees (usually 2/- a session) and provision of the books required. I served on the Joint Committee for Tutorial Classes at Reading almost from its initiation and I also conducted a Tutorial Class in English Literature* for twelve or fifteen years, when I resigned that work in favour of **MR H.V. DYSON**, lecturer in English, who carried it on most successfully until his departure to take up a post at Oxford in 1946.

It was the most difficult and some of the most invigorating work I have ever undertaken. I was quite accustomed to working-class audiences and had already lectured to every conceivable type of literary society and conducted a very large and keen evening class. But WEA teaching was something quite different and much more worthwhile. For one thing the work was continuous and systematic: the students were adults who brought to their studies a varied experience of life and knowledge of affairs. For another, their sole aim was to discover for themselves the delights of literature.

There was no question of any examination hallmark or of social advantage. These people craved admission to the fellowship of books of which they had hitherto for the most part been deprived. They came with no bias or preconceived notions of what they ought to admire or enjoy, and they asked for guidance, not for authority. Whole-hearted co-operation between tutor and class formed the basis of whatever was accomplished. The standard aimed at was that of the highest university honours work. I do not think

---

* Tutorial Classes were held in a variety of subjects – e.g. history, economics, and psychology. I speak only of my own experience, but other tutors give similar accounts.

it was often reached or possible of attainment except in rare instances. But something at least equally worthwhile was brought about: men and women whose school education had often ceased abruptly at the age of fourteen or even earlier were stimulated to use their minds for self-culture and to discover for themselves the pleasure to be derived from books and from abstract thought. They read and they wrote; they talked and argued; they acted themselves and we went together to see plays acted. We enjoyed together some fine literature, and many of them were set afire by the desire for more of the good things they had become aware of and learned to appreciate.

In the summer, when there was no weekly class meeting, small groups met to read together; the class collected a little library for its use; individual members began to fill their own bookshelves. I am convinced that to many of these men and women, life became richer and fuller because of their efforts to discover for themselves the joys of literature. Two or three students stand out in my memory as typical. There was a young man who came for many years. He had left school at fourteen and had endeavoured again and again to find assistance in the book-learning which he desired. Ultimately he succeeded in qualifying himself for a year's regular full-time attendance at the University, where he studied History and Philosophy as well as English Literature. He has resumed work at his trade, but in addition to the enrichment of his own life, his studies have qualified him to help younger men and women to enjoy similar pursuits.

Another outstanding pupil was a young cook who ultimately succeeded in gaining a scholarship at Ruskin (Working People's) College at Oxford, where she pursued her studies for the full course. Another notable student was the manageress of a Temperance Billiard Saloon. She had lived most of her life in a country village and had always longed for books and learning, but had had no opportunities and even believed she was different from other people in loving literature. To her, so she told me, the lectures opened a new world, and her response and intellectual development became an inspiration to all who came in contact with her. Groups of students met regularly in her room for discussion and reading: she collected books for herself and for the class, she read and she thought and she wrote, and she was in her sole person sufficient justification and proof of the success and wisdom of the WEA movement.

Class discussions with such eager students did not always terminate by the time when the University closed for the night and were often transferred to my own house and continued till eleven o'clock or later. Even when that was not the case, one or two people usually accompanied me home, and many of them formed the habit of dropping in at odd times for discussion of all sorts of questions. As recently as 1942, a former student, a man whom I had not seen for years, came to consult me on a personal difficulty, and with various of these students a bond has been made which will not easily be broken.

The Tutorial Classes are the most advanced work attempted by the WEA, but it also organises shorter and more elementary courses and single lectures and conferences lasting one day, a weekend, or for longer duration at Summer Schools up and down the country. In all these efforts I have been allowed to participate, and I am a convinced believer in the value of the movement. Reading University and its staff have always played an important part in co-operation with the local branch of the WEA and in this way also have felt they are promoting the ideas with which their founders were imbued, and are exerting influence on the welfare of the town in which they are situated.

One other semi-external university experience remains to be mentioned. In 1926 the Board of Education decided to terminate the centralised general examination for elementary teachers-in-training and determined that henceforth all Training Colleges should be affiliated to various universities which should be responsible for the awards of teaching diplomas to their students. Six such colleges asked for affiliation with Reading, and it became necessary to make plans for our association. We were only just emerging from our own dependence on external London examinations and were determined not to begin a relationship with the Training Colleges in which they were in a similar position of powerlessness to determine the syllabuses and educational policy desirable for their students. If we were to fix examination standards and to have the final authority in determining results, we must nevertheless ensure by some means or other that the teachers concerned played a vital part in the arrangements, and that we had first-hand knowledge of the colleges and students for whose examination we were to become responsible.

Eventually, most harmonious and satisfactory relations were established with benefit to all who participated in them. Boards of Study were constituted which consisted of all teachers of the particular subject concerned, together with the University representative or representatives. These Boards discussed and ratified syllabuses and examination papers: each college lecturer made a first draft of the proposed questions for his or her students, and these were criticised and passed by the University professor of the subject before final adoption. Each teacher also examined his own students' answers and made any suggestions and representations to the University examiner before the final decision was reached in individual cases.

Moreover, all those at the University responsible for the examination visited the colleges during the session, saw and lectured to the students and were present at some of the ordinary classes. In consequence the new arrangements worked smoothly and were, I believe, conducive to useful and enjoyable experiences on both sides; at any rate, I am very sure that in spite of the extra work involved this is very true in my own case. I shall always look back with pleasure to visits to Chichester, Culham, Brighton, Portsmouth and Salisbury which gave me a new understanding of the work and problems of the Training Colleges and brought new interests and friends.

CHAPTER 8:

Social and political activities

In 1908 I was definitely converted to socialism and joined the Fabian Society. Curiously enough, it was *News from Nowhere* which finally determined my conversion, a fact I thought peculiar to myself until Professor G.D.H. Cole told me, many years after, that for him too the final decision to become a socialist was made as a result of reading **MORRIS**'s idealistic rather than practical arguments. However, the attraction of the Fabian Society was precisely that it aimed at securing specific measures of social reform and that its primary object was to devise the various types of political machinery by which they could be carried out. Fabians were inspired by the belief that there was 'stuff at hand, plastic as they could wish' and that they

> Were called upon to exercise their skill,
> Not in Utopia, – subterranean fields, –
> Or some secreted island, Heaven knows where!
> But in the very world, which is the world
> Of all of us, – the place where, in the end,
> We find our happiness, or not at all!
> —W. Wordsworth, *French Revolution*

So the Fabian Society set out to permeate general opinion by the propagation of ideas about the reorganisation of society, or, in the words of its Basis, 'by the general dissemination of knowledge as to the relation between the individual and society in its economic, ethical and political aspects'. Facts were to be collected, checked and rechecked, irrespective of bias or preconceived notions. When they had been obtained and verified, they were to be broadcast and the resulting deductions drawn and presented in such a form that they could not be refuted. 'The Fabian Society consists of Socialists', but when there was no Labour Party and when the body of avowed socialists in this country was small and not politically important, Fabians were very ready to spread their ideas and to obtain their ends by means of any other party which could be induced to accept particular parts of their teaching.

This is not the place – nor am I the person – to write a history of the Fabian Society and the part it has played in the political developments of the sixty years of its existence[*] but I suppose that few would deny that it has exerted an influence altogether disproportionate to its small membership, and that many and various measures of reform introduced by all the parties have been brought about largely as a result of its research, its pamphlets and its teaching. To take only one example from its long list of publications, *Facts for Socialists, Showing the Distribution of the National Income and its Results*, a *6d.* tract which first appeared in 1887, was revised for its fourteenth edition in 1937[†] by which date 147,000 copies had already been distributed. The pamphlet consists chiefly of statistical tables with explanatory illustration. The effect is cumulative and the reader is left, in the main, to draw his own conclusions. One need but review recent bills and legislation to become aware of the effect of the published figures on the public conscience.

That the Fabians continue their work at the present time and are playing a full part in the investigation of contemporary problems may be proved by the titles of recent tracts such as *Your Coal and You, Food in War Time, Can We Afford Beveridge? The Assistance Board, Population Movements*

---

[*] See **E.R. PEASE**, *History of the Fabian Society* (1916) and G.D.H. Cole, *The Fabian Society* (1942).

[†] Fifteenth edition (1944), price 1/6.

and *The Colonies and Us.*[*] Nor can there be any question that there is still, and must always be, much work to be done by a body which devotes itself mainly to research, to the testing and discovery of truth, and thus to the provision of ammunition for speakers and politicians. The type of investigation undertaken may be illustrated by a small bit of work which was entrusted to myself.

The Fabian Women's Group was founded in 1908, chiefly with the object of studying the question of women's economic independence in relation to socialism. Its first task was to examine the history and facts concerning their position. At the height of the suffrage agitation, MABEL ATKINSON, my colleague at King's College for Women, herself a member of the Fabian Executive, produced a brilliant pamphlet for the group entitled *The Economic Foundations of the Women's Movement* in which she traced the changes which had taken place in the economic position of various classes of women as a result of the industrial revolution and the consequent abolition of the household as a unit of industry. 'Modern machinery and the use of artificial sources of power immensely cheapen production but they can be used only by organisations bigger than the family group … Inevitably this has reacted on the position of women'. Similarly, Miss Atkinson examined the changes which had driven middle-class women into the labour market and arrived at the conclusion that alterations in the whole fabric of society would be necessary if 'the normal woman' were 'to attain her twin demands [for] independent work and motherhood'.

Meanwhile the Group had set out to determine how far differences in ability for productive work were determined

[*] *Fabian Quarterly*, April 1944 (Diamond Jubilee Number) should be consulted for an account of the Society's work in the past, present and future.

by differences of sex function. It was necessary to investigate and establish or refute the possibility of women's economic independence and to determine what changes, if any, were desirable in order to facilitate its attainment. A series of lectures and discussions upon the subject was arranged and eventually these were summarised and published in two pamphlets, the first of which dealt with women not engaged in childbearing, the second with the special position and disabilities of mothers as wage-earners. Eminent authorities, medical and other, took part in the investigation, and evidence was also collected from women with practical, personal experience of various types of industrial work.

Next, about 1911, I was asked to edit a volume dealing on similar lines with the work and position of women engaged in the professions, and this was published shortly before the First World War, which at once produced new conditions that made it in some respects out-of-date. But *Women Workers in Seven Professions* remains of interest not merely from the historical point of view, and the picture it presents is still not altogether untrue to contemporary conditions, though these differ in various particulars from those prevailing in 1913. A quotation from the preface will serve to illustrate the fact that many problems then confronting the woman worker remain unsolved. It also proves that today's eager fighters for economic equality between the sexes are not the first in the field. The trail was blazed by the older generation whose work is often forgotten by those who are nowadays rightly calling out for the same things that their grandmothers and mothers were demanding.

> Almost all, as a result of their professional experience, definitely express the conviction that women need economic independence … . The writers are unanimous in their insistence upon the importance – to men as well as to women

– of equal pay for equal work, irrespective of sex. Wherever the subject of the employment of married women is mentioned – and it crops up in most of the papers – there is adverse comment on the economically unsound, unjust and racially dangerous tendency in many salaried professions to enforce upon women resignation on marriage. It is clear that professional women are beginning to show resentment at the attempt to force celibacy upon them.

Similarly, the 'Concluding Remarks' to the second of the pamphlets upon the disabilities of women as workers lay stress upon the need for co-operative nurseries and co-operative kitchens, and on the desirability of the specialised training of domestic workers. The plea for these things is made as much on behalf of the children and the home as of the housewives themselves.

> A mother for her own sake and for the sake of her children should have definite occupations and interests outside her home; … it is undesirable that she should attempt to rear her family unassisted.

There is also a demand for maternity benefit – not then in existence – and that 'the woman should be economically independent in virtue of her own exertions'.

MRS BERNARD SHAW, **MRS CHARLOTTE WILSON** and **MRS PEMBER REEVES** were the leading spirits and inspiration of the Women's Group of the Fabian Society in those days, and it was my good fortune, as a result of undertaking the editorship of the book they had sponsored, to be in close touch with them while the work was in progress. Later on, as a member of the Fabian Executive, I had the privilege of seeing how the leading spirits in the Society approached the problems which confronted them. It was an education to hear the **WEBBS**' insistence on the need for facts and the checking of facts. Their methods of investigation, their extraordinary, detailed knowledge of any and every economic subject which came up for discussion, their unfailing patience and untiring and completely impersonal and selfless labours set a standard before everyone with whom they came in contact.

Nor were they ever too busy to be on the lookout for new recruits, and 'the Webbs' young men' who have since made their mark in the economic field are there to justify and prove the force of their example. Among other then-members of the Executive were **E.R. PEASE**, historian and Hon. Secretary of the Society, **LAWSON DODD**, Treasurer, **EMIL DAVIES**, **R.K. ENSOR**, **MRS B. DRAKE**, St John Ervine, **CLIFFORD ALLEN**, Mabel Atkinson, **LETITIA FAIRFIELD**, **STEPHEN SANDERS**, **HARRY SNELL**, **MRS [E.C.] TOWNSHEND**, J.C. Squire, Mrs B. Shaw, Mrs Reeves and **SUSAN LAWRENCE**, so that it can be imagined that Executive meetings were provocative and inspiring occasions in which it was great good fortune to be allowed to participate.

But the Fabian Society was not always solemn, nor were its meetings designed solely for the promotion and extension of economic truth. On the contrary, great stress was laid upon social intercourse between its members, and it early discovered the method of acquiring 'strength through joy'.[65]

At any rate it was among the pioneer groups to inaugurate the 'Summer Schools' which have been a regular part

---

65 It is odd to see Morley use this phrase at the time she writes: it is the literal translation of the name of a German state-operated leisure organization ('Kraft durch Freude') whose aims were to provide workers with extensive recreational and travel opportunities, previously only available to the middle classes, in order to improve workers' physical health and productivity and gain control over the ways in which they spent their leisure time. It is possible that Morley uses the phrase inadvertently; after all, the Fabian summer schools served the purpose of 're-creation derived from wholesome enjoyment', as she says on p.106.

of its propaganda policy since July 1907, when the first was held at Llanbedr near Barmouth. These Schools have deliberately subordinated formal lectures and study to the equally important business of uniting members from the central and local Fabian organisations and of teaching them to work and mix together.

Informal discussion during open air activities, debates and conferences add to normal holiday pleasures and often lead to the discovery of talents not hitherto suspected either by their possessors or by the leaders of the Society, who are thus enabled to make profitable use of them in the work that Fabians have at heart. Moreover these School gatherings are genuinely democratic in their composition. People of all ages and of every variety of circumstances and occupation live a common life on equal and friendly terms. To see G.B.S. [George Bernard Shaw] take his turn at washing up plates, or cheerfully fielding at cricket with a set of youngsters – invariably courteous, provided no-one attempted to lionise him – or to go climbing with Olivier;[66] to do physical jerks with Lawson Dodd or Emil Davies; these things break down reticence and shyness and definitely contribute to the understanding of democratic living in practice.

A 'director' was responsible for the programme of the week and, though the formal daily lectures were arranged in advance, it was his business to get up all the informal discussions, debates, excursions and entertainments, of which the Friday night party was the chief. But for more than twenty years **MARY HANKINSON**, Secretary of the Ling Association,[67]

66 Sydney Haldane Olivier was an Oxford-educated civil servant, politician and author. He had several secretarial and governmental posts in the colonies and was a strong advocate of reforming the Empire. In 1885 he joined the Fabian Society, where he was Secretary 1886–9.

67 The Ling Association was formed in 1899 to bring together teachers of Swedish Gymnastics in the British Isles. It became the Physical Education Association of the UK, and later the Association for Physical Education.

acted as 'manager', i.e. responsible housekeeper throughout the month of August when the School was normally held, and what 'Hanky' said was law to great and small. She ruled with a rod of iron, or rather by the affection she inspired, and she was the life and soul of all the doings of the School. Her recitations were among the perennial joys. I think her repertoire consisted of only three pieces, but these were called for again and again, and she could always get a thrill with her 'goblins will have *you* if you don't watch out'.[68] Other times, other manners.

The day came when the younger generation demanded more freedom to go their own way about such weighty matters as locking-up hours and the like than Hanky thought possible to concede without danger to the Society's reputation. But their elders will not easily forget what Hanky achieved in building up that reputation in days when all 'socialists' were suspect as 'atheists' and loose livers. Nor will they forget the many pleasant holidays at home and abroad in which she saved them all the troubles of arrangement and planning, and ministered to their spiritual, mental and physical requirements.

In connection with the Fabian School, I recall a few lighter incidents that may be worth recording. During the First World War, I think in the summer of 1917, we were at Pen Lee near Dartmouth. Wednesdays were reserved for whole-day expeditions, and on one very warm August day we had been in the open, walking, cycling, etc. from morning to evening (I was with a party which missed its way, and we had walked over twenty-five miles!). After dinner, Shaw was to lecture to the assembled company on Ireland, and we were to listen in a close room too small for the company and,

68 A (mis)quote from *Little Orphant Annie* (1885) by James Whitcomb Riley: 'An' the Gobble-uns 'at gits you/Ef you/Don't/Watch/Out!'

since it faced the sea, rigidly blacked out. G.B.S. announced that his lecture was prepared and he meant to deliver it even if everyone in the audience, including the chairman (myself), fell asleep. The lecture has since been published and subsequently most of its recommendations and conclusions have been accepted by successive governments. It may therefore be assumed that its words of wisdom were worth attention. But one by one the hearers rolled off their uncomfortable chairs and benches in the stuffy room, and I believe Shaw himself kept awake only because he was on his legs and talking. It was the funniest sight imaginable to watch his somnolent audience's vain endeavour to keep awake – nor were my own eyes watchful all the time.

Another – to me – very memorable occasion was when **ARTHUR HENDERSON** came to lecture to us at Frensham Heights, and I was asked afterwards to drive him and Sidney Webb back to Passfield Corner. It was an August Bank Holiday and I was a new and inexperienced driver. Well do I recollect my inward tremors at being entrusted with the safety of the then leaders of the Labour Party. Happily there is nothing further to relate about the incident.

A memory of another kind is of the occasion when James Elroy Flecker declaimed for us parts of his still unpublished *Hassan*. There were also many evenings when Shaw read aloud his plays, usually those then still unpublished. And many less distinguished writers followed his example and first tried out the effect of their work on their fellow Fabians. Nor, finally, can I bear to leave unrecorded the hilarious fancy dress parties, the performances brilliantly staged by Mrs Basil Hall, and the mock trials in which leading legal luminaries took part. All these things, as well as the more serious lectures and discussions, rendered these holidays memorable, in addition to the contacts formed with many and varied people of distinction, both British and foreign.

Inevitably my increased knowledge of Fabian social and economic investigations strengthened my already lively interest in the movement for women's suffrage. While an undergraduate at University College I had signed for the first time a petition for the conferment of the vote, and my conviction of the need for this symbol of full citizenship had grown with my growth and interest in public affairs. I do not wish to write in detail of the long fight; the best and fullest account of the movement is to be found in *The Cause* by **RAY STRACHEY**,[69] whose admirable, temperate and just description should be consulted by all those who are interested in the subject. What I have to say is only from the personal experience of a consistent supporter who, though she played an insignificant part in the struggle, nevertheless came into personal contact with most of the prominent, active participants and their opponents.

In the first place I desire to place it on record that there is no truth in the charge that either suffragists or suffragettes were sex-thwarted, hysterical seekers after notoriety. Indeed, how could this have been so, since the vast majority of women and practically all women workers of every type and social grade were convinced supporters of the claim for political rights. In my own fairly large circle I had but two friends and one acquaintance who professed themselves to be anti-suffragists, though of course there were many who took no active part in the controversy. The main body of women opposed to the change was composed of those who led sheltered lives and had small experience of or interest in public affairs.

Secondly, it is untrue that the leaders, whether of the 'polites' (suffragists) or suffragettes, were moved by purely personal reasons or enjoyed the notoriety or publicity they acquired. Personally, I came across one such woman among

69   *The Cause: A short history of the women's movement in Great Britain* (1928)

the younger leaders, and of her I think it is fair criticism to say that her head was turned by her success as a speaker. I met and knew most of the other leaders, many of them happily married to men who supported their views: they were for the most part earnest, mature women whose experience of life and social and economic conditions had convinced them of the need for both sexes to play their part as full citizens and active co-operators. 'Feminists' we were, but emphatically not in the sense of being foolish and unnatural opponents of the other sex.

No doubt some women are man-haters, as some men are misogynists – but these are the perverted minority and it was not of such that the bulk of suffragists was composed. A great deal of nonsense was talked in the heat of controversy about the deleterious effects political equality between the sexes would have upon normal human relationships. In fact there does not appear to be any change, or likelihood of change, in the interest men and women take in each other, nor would any sane person wish to see confusion between the functions of the two sexes, which are complementary not antagonistic. But important and pervasive as sex and its attributes are, this cannot be a reasonable ground for the refusal of full citizenship and its responsibilities, whether political or economic.

The acute phase of the suffrage movement lasted for some eight or nine years immediately before the outbreak of the First World War in 1914. Though I was precluded by my position and temperament from active participation in the doings of the suffragettes, I belonged to the WSPU[70] and subscribed to their funds. Much as, on principle, I dislike

70 The Women's Social and Political Union was the leading militant organisation campaigning for women's suffrage. It was founded by the PANKHURSTS in 1903. Their motto was 'Deeds not words', and their campaigning included the disruption of political meetings, threats to public order and, finally, attacks on property.

acts of violence and illegal methods, I still think that but for their efforts we should have waited much longer than we did for the successful outcome of the agitation for the vote, since it was made obvious by actual happenings that successive governments were not to be moved by legal and constitutional methods. Nor was the violence all on the part of the women, who suffered much worse than they inflicted or could inflict.

Several lighter incidents, as they affected myself, arose out of the conflict. In the thirty-nine years of my active connection with Reading College and University, once – and only once – was I absent on an important ceremonial occasion. This was when Lord Haldane, then Secretary for War, came to open the Hall in October 1906. He consented to officiate on condition that no woman, whether on the staff or student, was present at the ceremony; for no Minister at that time felt safe from suffragette interruptions.

On another occasion I was refused admittance to the railway station when on the way to London. My protest was met by the answer that Asquith was expected by the next train and that until his safe departure from the railway no known suffragette – I wore the WSPU badge – could be admitted. In vain my statement that I had an important engagement to keep in town; in vain that I pointed out that my train departed five minutes before his was due. Only after an interview with the station master was I allowed on to the departure platform, to wait between two guards until seen safely on to my train. Even that experience was less disagreeable than the occasion when some of my property was publicly sold by auction (and bought in and returned to me by the sympathetic auctioneer) in default of payment of rates – a form of resistance adopted as a protest against taxation without representation. Most of the students of the College assembled to hear the preliminary street-corner orations and were present at the sale. It was a most uncongenial business, and one I suffered as a minor martyrdom.

More amusing was an unsought-for experience at Aldeburgh, where I had gone for a pleasant weekend with a friend. It was when census resisting had been widely advertised as a means of protest. On a visit to a conventional household, the head of which was Mayor of the town, I had no thought of participation in the resistance. But on arrival, I found my friend had thoughtfully arranged for me to spend the night marching up and down the parade with **DR GARRETT ANDERSON** so that neither of us would have to be set down as sleeping in a house!

Nor must I forget 'my' first letter to *The Times*. **MRS PANKHURST** wanted publicity for some aspect of the suffrage question and wrote a letter which she thought my title might get accepted. So signing it with my initials only, I obediently copied and sent it off. On the day it appeared, someone from *The Times* appeared at the College for an interview. He was told I was in London that morning. And there about noon I was called downstairs to meet the representative of the paper who wished for my views on the momentous question. When he heard I was the Professor Morley he had taken so much trouble to track down, his language was not exactly parliamentary: 'Sold again' and a bang on the table were his parting shots as he stormed out of the room without troubling to elicit my opinions.

Or there was the occasion when, in one of the organised processions through London, a friendly policeman helped carry my banner from Baker Street to the Albert Hall (the London force were mostly friendly to the women; provincial police had to be called on when physical violence was used against them). Finally, there was the momentous evening when **MRS FAWCETT** and many other eager women, myself among them, awaited the result of the Commons' vote, only to hear their Bill had been 'torpedoed' by the Prime Minister.

Was all the agitation worthwhile? The answer is emphatically 'Yes'. The vote has not brought the millennium nor did anyone sensible suppose that it would. But as we expected, it has proved the lever by which many changes have been made possible. It was, for example, a new experience for women to find that their representations to Members of Parliament gained serious attention; that candidates listened to what they had to say about proposed or desired legislation; that they could make their influence felt in all sorts of ways hitherto debarred to them. Nor was it long before responsible citizenship brought women new duties in its train. For the first time they sat on juries, they became magistrates, they were elected members of the House of Commons and served on important committees. Much remains to be accomplished before complete political, social and economic equality is achieved, but no woman who grew up in Victorian conditions can hesitate about her answer if asked whether the position of women has improved since the nineteenth century and whether the improvement is or is not bound up with the successful outcome of the suffrage agitation.

When war broke out in 1914, the agitation was suspended for the time being, much to the relief of all concerned. Men and women united in service to the country, and, to the manifest surprise of the authorities, they discovered that their *quondam* opponents were in the forefront when reliable help from women was asked. The Women's Emergency Corps[71] was at once organised, mainly by suf-

---

71 The Women's Emergency Corps was founded by WSPU member Evelina Haverfield and actress Decima Moore in 1914 to aid the war effort. It encouraged women to volunteer their services in a range of fields to replace men who had enlisted, and it helped to organise their employment.

fragists who as time went on also took leading parts in every description of war work open to them. Then, as now, a great deal of nonsense was talked about the women being 'magnificent'. Naturally and properly, they emulated their husbands, sons, fathers and brothers in proving themselves to be loyal and patriotic citizens. In the present war, having achieved full citizenship, the privilege and duty of service is theirs equally with men. Their efforts should be recognised with similar gratitude but without the fulsome praise which seems to bespeak previous doubts on the part of those who utter it. As Mrs Poyser[72] long ago remarked, and it is true in a good as well as in a bad sense, the Almighty made women to match the men.

It was during the First World War that it dawned on the authorities, not without considerable prompting from women themselves, that they could set men free for naval and military duties by undertaking many types of work in civilian life and behind the front line. Various Ministries, especially those newly established, welcomed women's collaboration: women eagerly responded when urged to become munition workers, they drove lorries and worked as postwomen, omnibus conductors, on the railway, even as engineers, and, of course, were admitted to banks and to every kind of non-official office and business. Finally, the Women's Auxiliary Services[73] were established, and uniformed women, in addition to nurses, VADs [Voluntary Aid Detachment] etc. penetrated to the various theatres of war. That WRNSs [Women's Royal Naval Service], WAACs [Women's Army Auxiliary Corps] and WRAFs [Women's Royal Air Force] made good is amply proved, if further

72 A character in George Eliot's first novel, *Adam Bede* (1859).

73 The Women's Auxiliary Force was launched in 1915. It was a voluntary organisation of uniformed part-time workers who worked on the land, in hospitals and in canteens. It also provided social clubs.

proof is needed, by the way in which they were immediately re-established without hesitation at the outbreak of hostilities in 1939. The original Women's Auxiliary Forces were not conscripted even when conscription was introduced for men later on: they and their civilian sister-workers were on trial and their services more tentatively accepted in those days, though quite as eagerly offered as now. Never again could it be said that British women were incapable of public service or that 'Men must work while women must weep': they proved their right to full citizenship by the parts they played during the war years. When the vote was at last accorded in 1918 (at first only to women over thirty), it seemed almost an anticlimax, so much had it come to be regarded as a matter of course even by the most violent opponents to this extension of the suffrage. When universal suffrage was introduced a few years later, all men and women of twenty-one and over obtained the vote on equal terms and practically without adverse discussion.

As I have said, I remained at my own post throughout the war years, but, like everyone else, I filled my spare time with as many odds and ends of public work as I could manage. Among these the following deserve mention for one reason or another.

The Ministry of Food enrolled speakers to impress the need to 'eat less bread', and there was one terrible occasion when I was asked to go to a cinema on a half holiday afternoon to interrupt the show, crowded with soldiers and munition workers, with a brief exhortation on this subject. I still think the time and place ill-chosen, for then as now the Forces had all they required in rations, and in any case, the middle of a performance was an unsuitable occasion for a homily. I was given two or three points that were to be made and advised not to allow a spotlight to be turned on me. The latter warning proved necessary, for the obliging manager at once suggested that I should speak to a darkened auditorium with a light picking me out. When the lights went up, the audience were unprepared and angry. Men with their best girls on their knees; women suckling their babies; hooligans of every kind: they booed and hissed and made catcalls as soon as they took in the reason for my presence. It was the worst experience I have ever had as a speaker, and I can but be thankful that it made me angry and therefore obstinately determined not to be put off by the clamour. After various attempts, I managed to shout that I was not going until I had said my say, and that the sooner they let me speak my few sentences, the sooner they would get rid of me. They quietened down after that, and ended by becoming as friendly as they had been hostile so that I departed amid a round of applause. When I reached my bicycle, I found I was shaking from head to foot, and I could not mount until I had walked a considerable distance. I sincerely hope I may never again have to undergo a similar ordeal for which experience of academic lecturing had given me no training! All other addresses on the same subject, or lectures to the Forces, were child's play in comparison with that awful quarter of an hour.

Another terrible experience, very different in kind, was meeting trainloads of Belgian refugees in London and helping to conduct them to Alexandra Palace and elsewhere. That came in the early days of the war, when British civilians were quite unacclimatised to horrors, and the shocks and bewilderment of hitherto unknown conditions added to the misery of realising what 'total war' entailed. However awful our present-day experiences, at any rate no-one was unprepared, as we were in 1914, for what would have to be endured, since even the young today have grown up with a knowledge and expectation of suffering which the older generation had been spared. *Their* world, alas, has never been secure. *We* had no conception of its instability and in that respect, at any rate, the first catastrophe was more overwhelming than the second, which had not and could not have the same effect of unexpectedness. The Belgian refugees brought me my first unforgettable realisation of the meaning of war to those who had suffered the invasion of a ruthless enemy. In those years, as at present, one effect of the war was the weakening of moral sanctions and a natural unloosing of evil tendencies. If life was to be short, at least it should be unrestrained, and there was, especially among the undisciplined, a wild desire to 'be merry' (there was not much chance to overeat and drink), 'for tomorrow we die'. Then, as recently, police forces were depleted; youth movements were non-existent in their most attractive forms; Scouts and Guides[74] for example had not yet come into being; clubs for boys and girls had lost many of their best helpers, and the streets were dark and offered many opportunities not to be found elsewhere for unbridled behaviour.

Many people felt that there was a great opportunity for preventive work, and already in October 1914 the National Council of Women[75] inaugurated, as an emergency war service, the system of Voluntary Patrols[76] which gradually spread all over the country. By the end of the war some 5000

---

74 Contrary to what Morley says, the Scouts were formed in 1908, the Girl Guides in 1910.

75 The National Council of Women of Great Britain was founded in 1895 as the National Union of Women Workers (NUWW) in response to unsatisfactory working conditions experienced by many women at the time. It quickly developed into a nationwide network of small groups and acted as an umbrella organisation. Within two years it had become affiliated to the International Council of Women.

76 These voluntary patrols saw themselves as aides to the established police. They spent a great deal of time walking the streets, patrolling parks and public spaces, separating courting couples and attempting to prevent immoral behaviour among young women.

of these Patrols had demonstrated that there was a permanent place for women in the Police Forces. Meanwhile I had been approached to know whether something could be done in Reading and, as the need was obvious, I made enquiries about possible volunteers. Ultimately some couple of dozen or more women in the town undertook to carry out the simple instructions issued. We had no powers or authority; all we could do was to exert what influence was possible by our presence and readiness to help or, if necessary, to report to the police.

The method was to parade in couples from eight to ten every evening: we wore armlets which, it was hoped, would look official to the uninitiated, and each patrol carried a lantern. Our instructions were never to talk to a male offender or to any woman known to be a professional prostitute. If possible we were to advise and warn giddy girls when they were not in company with men. If objectionable 'love-making' appeared to be going on, we were to walk up and down silently, *but with the lantern*, and it was commonly found that this procedure was not conducive to billing and cooing. We also watched and reported on houses which appeared to be frequented for immoral purposes, and we observed whether children were sent to fetch drinks from public houses. The job was not pleasant but there is no doubt it was useful.

For example, it was on one occasion necessary to have two girls arrested in order to frighten them. We had, in fact, sufficient evidence to bring them before the court, but we had no intention of instituting proceedings. We were acting on advice given by a sympathetic police officer the night before, for this pair had given persistent trouble for days and needed a sharp lesson. But on the evening in question the constable, when at last found half a mile from the place where the offence was committed, was not our friend of the previous night and was the reverse of helpful. He refused to allow us to meet him there, but insisted we should accompany him and the girls, now shrieking and crying, the three-quarters of a mile to the police station. Nor was our interview with the charge-officer very pleasant. Finally, having obtained the girls' names and addresses, we were given five minutes' start of them to make ourselves scarce. We escaped them all right, but it was a nasty quarter of an hour! When the cases were followed up, the mother of one of the culprits was more than grateful for our intervention; the other came from a less respectable home. But the remarkable result of the arrest was the immediate improvement of girls' behaviour in the streets, so that for weeks afterwards there was no further trouble with them.

Meanwhile representatives of the Women Patrols, much against the will of the then Chief Constable of Reading, secured an interview with the Watch Committee, to whom they gave evidence of their experiences and of their views upon the need for women police, especially as they were themselves unable, after two years, to continue their voluntary service. Very soon after, two full-time, paid women police officers were appointed, and from that time women have regularly served in the Reading force. Today it has at last become the policy of the Home Office to sanction and encourage a considerable increase in the number of fully-trained policewomen throughout Great Britain and not least in the country districts.[*]

[*] Since 1916 it has been permissible to pay full-time policewomen out of the Police Grant, but they could not be sworn in until 1919, when the Sex Disqualification (Removal) act was passed and the appointment of women as police constables was thereby legalised. However, it was not until April 1944 that the various police authorities were required by the then Home Secretary to consider as a matter of urgency the provision, or further provision, of policewomen or attested women auxiliaries. HM Inspectors of Constabulary were asked to advise how many policewomen should be employed so that the establishment for each area might be fixed by the Home Secretary instead of being left to the option of the local Police Authorities.

One result of the experience of the Patrols was that it very soon became obvious to myself and others that something more than prevention of misbehaviour was required if young men and women were to be kept out of temptation. They needed opportunities for social intercourse in attractive and decent surroundings where they could enjoy each other's society without coming to harm. So we opened a Recreation Club for Men and Women were they could dance, play billiards, read and write, or listen to good music as well as obtain inexpensive and palatable refreshment. It amazes me to remember how much opposition the scheme encountered from 'old women' of both sexes. One worthy but old-fashioned worker among girls told me that I was destroying the morals of the town by the encouragement of dancing. When I asked whether the good lady thought it an immoral pastime, she replied quite seriously that she had no objection to the 'exercise', provided men and women danced in separate rooms!

We were very fortunate in securing the services of an enlightened ex-Baptist missionary as (most inadequately) paid superintendent of the Club. His dog-collar gave it the required air of respectability, and to him and the canteen manager (also very inadequately remunerated) the entire success of the new venture was in great measure due. A large and regular rota of voluntary helpers also had to be organised, and an active committee to take responsibility. I served as Honorary Secretary throughout the four years of the club's existence, and it was in spite of valiant efforts that we finally closed down, because our rented premises were bought by another organisation while we were endeavouring to collect the large sum necessary for purchase. No other suitable accommodation could be obtained so the venture had to come to an end, but not before it had completely justified its existence.

There was an average of 12,000 attendances per month which filled the club to capacity: it was opened each weekday from 6.30pm and on Sundays from 3.30 until 10pm, and men and women flocked there for recreation and relaxation of every kind. The demand for and possibilities of such a club for adults above the age of eighteen were palpable, and personally I have long been convinced, by my experience of what could be achieved in war conditions, of the desirability of the extension of club facilities in every urban and rural centre. No doubt there are various ways of meeting the need, by community centres as well as by clubs, but that provision for wholesome recreation together in pleasant surroundings is an urgent necessity for men and women of all ages admits of no question. I hope the day has at last dawned when club premises will be regarded as a necessary part of every building scheme in the country. A very small weekly subscription from members should enable them to become self-supporting once the buildings and furniture are provided, and with a stable membership the clubs could be managed entirely by the people frequenting them. Different kinds of recreation would be necessary for different types of member, but all alike require opportunity for relaxation and social intercourse from which a majority of decent citizens are debarred in present circumstances.[*] I have no hesitation in asserting that our Recreation Club for Men and Women met a genuine need, and that the town suffered a real loss when it came to an end through no fault either of its promoters or frequenters. To this day nothing has arisen to take its place and fill the gap caused by its disappearance. During the recent war and since the conclusion of hostilities, in spite of all the efforts of YMCA, YWCA and similar admirable

[*]   Cf. on this point the evidence given in *The Peckham Experiment* by Innes Pearse and Lucy Crocker (1943).

institutions, the streets afford eloquent testimony to the absence of adequate opportunities for social intercourse. While the need is greater when many people are forced by war conditions into unfamiliar surroundings, it exists permanently and is a cause of unexpressed, often unrealised suffering to many men and women who lack facilities for forming friendships and gaining fresh interests outside the four walls of their homes.

Many years after the end of hostilities in 1918, my conviction of the desirability of providing opportunity for outside interests, especially for those whose main occupations were domestic, caused me to take part in another movement. This was that of the Townswomen's Guilds, whose objects are to encourage women's education as citizens contributing to the common good, and to give them opportunities for social intercourse. We got the Reading Townswomen's Guild going some ten years ago, and it flourishes exceedingly, with an enthusiastic membership of several hundreds. The Guild meets monthly for lectures, music, play readings, whist and bridge drives, and the meetings usually include 'A Social Half-hour' arranged by members, and a trading stall. The members are of very varied social rank and occupation, and they undertake divers tasks together to their mutual benefit. Personally I no longer take part in the proceedings but I know from more active members that the Guild is fulfilling for town-dwellers similar functions to those of the Women's Institutes in rural districts. The number of such Guilds is now large, and there is no doubt of their value to the community.

A more important part has been played in my own life by the influence and varied activities of the British Federation of University Women [BFUW]. This was first founded in 1907 in Manchester, and I became one of the original members of the London Association when it came into being shortly after. The Federation consists of women who have enjoyed the privileges of a university education and who, whatever their subsequent experience, whether in the home or in the exercise of a profession, must therefore necessarily have certain interests in common. By combining as members of their National Federation, women are able, through the Central Executive, 'to play an active and effective part in promoting such interests' and to take concerted action in matters of importance which affect them. At present there are more than thirty Associations in the British Federation and these are engaged in a great variety of useful work of municipal and local importance.* In addition, through the Central Executive (on which each local Association is represented) they are enabled to take a share in wider issues which concern them all. For example, the Academic Sub-Committee is mainly concerned with the provision and award of postgraduate fellowships which enable research work of various kinds to be undertaken by qualified persons who would not otherwise have means or leisure for its completion. The Parliamentary and Public Relations Sub-Committee are concerned with such matters as the successful campaign for Equal Compensation for War Injuries; the question of the admission of women to the reformed Foreign Service and to the Colonial Service; the inclusion of an adequate number of qualified women on government committees; the nationality of married women, etc. etc. The Emergency Sub-Committee for Refugees plays a vital part in the assistance of women graduates who are refugees from Nazi oppression;

---

* The Reading Association was formed in the year 1925, and for many years I acted as its Honorary Secretary and representative on the Central Executive. I also served as its President from 1937 to 1940, until which date I was continually on the local committee. We began with a very small membership which has now grown to some 110, representing at least fourteen different universities.

the name of the Committee on International Relations explains the nature of its work, as does that of the Sub-Committee on Reconstruction of Libraries. The Association is also represented on such bodies as the Joint Committee to Investigate the Health of Women Workers in Bad Climates, the Ministry of Information Advisory Panel, WVS [Women's Voluntary Service] and the like. At the present time, 'The Professional Woman and Social Reconstruction' is a subject of outstanding interest, and a half-day conference to debate some of its aspects was organised and most successfully held under the auspices of the Federation in November 1943. Thirty-six other societies were also represented at the conference, which was widely attended. The main topics discussed were 'Planning for Social Security' and 'Town and Country Planning', both matters of immediate and intrinsic importance.

It was not until after the foundation of the International Federation of University Women [IFUW] in 1920 that the most far-reaching influence of the BFUW became felt. The International Federation was one result of the British University Mission to the USA in 1918. Professor Spurgeon, a member of the Mission, was deeply imbued with a sense of the importance of good relations between the universities of the two countries, and, finding that American women graduates were also united in a federation, in discussion with **DEAN GILDERSLEEVE** of Columbia University she conceived the idea of an international federation of university women of all countries 'to do what we can to see that such a war never happens again'. That ultimate object, alas, was not attained. But the International Federation came into being and held its inaugural conference at Bedford College in 1920, when Professor Spurgeon was unanimously elected its first President.

The seed sown grew and flourished so that when Hitler came into power, it boasted no fewer than twenty-six constituent national federations as members. Individuals belonging to any such national federation automatically became members of the IFUW, the main work of which was and is to establish as many friendly international contacts as possible between university women, the mothers and teachers of coming generations. In peace time, international conferences were held every three or four years in different countries, e.g. at Oslo, Amsterdam, Edinburgh, Geneva, Cracow, Stockholm, and at these there assembled several hundreds of university women from all over the world to transact business, to confer and debate on a variety of subjects of general interest and, above all, to make friends and hear each other's points of view.

Many promising steps have been taken as a result of the International Federation. For example, various international research fellowships have been established which are open to members of any national federation and tenable in any other country than that of the holder. The work done by the recipients has been of the most varied kind, the only similarity being in the excellence of its quality. Each national Federation selects its own candidates from those who desire to submit applications to the international awarding committee, and often the difficulty is to decide between the many excellent claimants. It is consequently a primary need to endow more of these fellowships so that good work may not be impeded by lack of funds.

Another valuable step was taken by the establishment of International Club Houses for university women in various countries. The first of these to be set up in Europe was Reid Hall, the American centre in Paris.[77] Next, Crosby Hall was founded as a residential and non-residential club in Chelsea

---

77 Originally an American Girls' Club set up by Mrs Elisabeth Mills Reid, in 1922 she began converting the complex to house a centre for advanced and university studies for American women.

on the site originally occupied by another home of Sir Thomas More who, for a short period, had owned Crosby Hall in Bishopsgate. The beautiful Hall had been transported for another purpose from its original home in the City and rebuilt stone by stone in its new position. It was Professor Spurgeon who first determined that the Hall should become the nucleus of a new home for women graduates, and with the support of other enthusiasts, notably **MRS ALYS RUSSELL** and **PROFESSOR WINIFRED CULLIS**, the dream became a reality. No less than £50,000 had to be collected for the purchase of the fabric and for the erection of the residential wing, but by 1926 the task was achieved and the building ready for occupation. On 2nd July 1927 HM Queen Mary declared the Hall open for residence, in the presence of 800 guests, including the Ambassadors and Ministers of all the countries represented in the IFUW, and of Professor Gledhow of Oslo University, at that time President of the Federation:

> The purpose of Crosby Hall, with its adjuncts, is to be an International Hall of Residence for University Women', graduates of all countries who come to London to carry on research or other post-graduate work. 'University women in all professions and from all parts of the civilised world … foregather in such scholarly friendship as, on a smaller scale, prevailed in More's house in Chelsea.

By the devoted and enlightened services of the first Warden, Miss Spurling, the residential part of the Hall speedily became a much sought-after temporary home; the beautiful old Hall with its glorious oriel window was in daily use for meals and receptions, the two common rooms and library served as club rooms for non-resident as well as resident members, while both the BFUW and IFUW had their central offices on the premises. When the blitz came in 1940, the Hall had to be temporarily closed, though happily it was not seriously damaged. It stood empty until, in

1943, it was decided that the offices should return to their old quarters and part of the building be used for club purposes, and especially for the gatherings of the International Federation which the presence of so many foreign graduates in London made more desirable than ever. At that moment the Admiralty decided to requisition the whole building for use by the WRNS and thus, for the time being, it passed from the possession of the Federation. But in the summer of 1946 all members rejoiced at the re-opening for its original functions as one of the longed-for results of the end of hostilities.

Meanwhile the offices found a new temporary abode in King's Road, Chelsea, where, happily, there is a small hall for meetings and debates. Various important conferences on reconstruction problems have taken place and to these many of our foreign friends have made important contributions. American, French, Czech, Polish, Greek, Italian, Swedish, Austrian and German women graduates have all taken part in the discussions, and we have even had the unexpected pleasure of a visit from the Swedish Vice-President of the International Federation, **DR KOCK**, who was able to give us first-hand information of the impact and results of war in her own country. The present President of the International, a Pole, managed to continue work in Cracow throughout the occupation and is now once more in touch with her colleagues in other countries. In the summer of 1943 we heard from various constituent members, e.g. that

> Much relief work continues to be carried on in Sweden and in Switzerland. Mexico is hard at work developing a growing programme ... Palestine has sent in a resolution of protest against Nazi atrocities and continues to help many refugees. India, too, has had much opportunity for assisting refugees from the Far East. The newly formed Federation of Ceylon ... is busy studying a proposal for the

establishment of a Domestic Science College on the island. The President of the Argentine Federation has reported the formation of a new Federation in Bolivia as a result of her visit there.

This quotation from the organ of the BFUW (*The University Women's Review*, June 1943) serves to illustrate the scope of the International Federation and to indicate some of the varied interests and enterprises of university women throughout the world. They held fast to their faith that even in the midst of the horrors of war they could prepare for the resumption and extension of that intellectual co-operation between thinking people in all countries which is the only sure basis of durable peace. In July 1946, Crosby Hall once again was able to welcome the members of the Council of the IFUW at their first meeting since the outbreak of war.

The British Federation is also full of life, and while individual members are as much occupied as everyone else these days, the Executive yet manages to cope with the greatly increased volume of business which is of importance for women today and in the future. At any rate I personally am convinced of the outstanding reasons why all university women graduates should be members of the Federation. To them individually it is a means of expanding interests and friendships. Especially if their work calls them into new surroundings, it keeps them in touch with people of their own kind and gives them the required social contacts. But over and above personal benefits to be derived from membership, each subscription to a local Association means an increase to central funds and is a contribution to the variety of useful work the Federation undertakes. Moreover, 'unity is strength', and experience proves that the united influence of educated women can be exerted for the promotion of good causes both at home and abroad.

CHAPTER 9:

The last chapter

The date of my retirement, Michaelmas 1940, and the fact that I was still well and active, precluded the thought of devoting my leisure solely to literary research, also made difficult by the bar upon travel which prevented frequent visits to libraries. So I at once set about the search for useful employment, if possible in connection with the war effort. It took me a long time to realise that voluntary service from a woman of my age was not welcomed by the authorities. Though I offered myself in any capacity, however humble, in which I could be useful to each of the Ministries temporarily located in Reading, I was told that only paid officers could be employed. When I pointed out that I had no insuperable objection to the receipt of a salary, I was told of posts carrying a payment of £250–£300 a year. While I was fully prepared and anxious for unpaid work, it was obviously impossible for me to accept a salary suited to an untrained girl, so my endeavours came to nothing. The only suggestion made to me was by the Ministry of Information, that I should go round to various Women's Institutes to talk to members on 'The Home Front', i.e. about household saving in cookery and the like, a subject about which they were much better informed than myself.

Eventually I was invited to serve on the Ministry of Labour Domestic Hardships Advisory Panel, and this I was glad to do when occasion offered. I also gave occasional lectures to the Forces. During the session 1941–2 I was invited by a former colleague, now Professor of English Literature at the University of Liverpool, to assist him temporarily owing to the depletion of his staff. As a result, from October to the end of May I went up north once a fortnight from

Sunday to Wednesday and enjoyed the advantage of acquaintance with the inside working of another university. I gave six lectures to various classes each visit, so that with the long journey each way it was a rather gruelling experience. It was however a real pleasure to be engaged once more in the work for which I felt fitted, and I was sorry when it had to come to an end because full-time assistance was needed. Doubtless it is a low taste, but I really enjoy lecturing and teaching even when I have no responsibility for the students concerned. Moreover it was a great pleasure to mix once more in academic circles with people sharing my own interests.

Reading was a reception area during the air raids of 1940, and for about a year I helped with work among the evacuees, taking children to their billets, visiting billetees and their hosts, distributing dinner tickets and doing odd jobs of clerical work at a community centre and the like. But none of this sufficed to provide adequate occupation, and I could not feel that my services were of much value or that they could not have been rendered by anyone without my training or experience. Fortunately for myself there were two bits of work which had already presented themselves before my retirement and to which I was now able to devote more attention. I had been made a magistrate in 1934 and found the duties it entailed of absorbing interest.

Long before that date, while still quite a young woman, I had joined the Howard League and had ever since kept up my interest in penal reform. Now I was enabled to come into personal contact with the workings of the law and with transgressors and the penalties they incurred, as well as with various types of remedial work in connection with them. I have never served on the Juvenile Panel, but as a member of the Probation Committee it is possible for me to have close contact with the methods and results of the probation system and with the officers to whom its work is entrusted. The business of care and training of offenders is full of interest and is among the most promising of social enterprises, and I regard it as a real privilege to be able to take a small share in what is being done.

Then, at the end of 1938, I was asked by a cousin in Liverpool who was responsible for housing and looking after refugee students at the University there, whether I could do anything to help a young German Jew for whom a free place was required in an agricultural college. Was there any possibility of his admission as a student at the University of Reading? I asked our Vice-Chancellor, found him most sympathetic and helpful, and eventually by his assistance three free places annually were secured at Reading for refugees from Nazi oppression. In this way my own interest was aroused in the subject of help to these victims of Hitler's tyranny. I approached the then Mayor of Reading, Councillor McIlroy,[78] and suggested he might possibly sponsor a meeting and help form a local Refugee Committee. Through him I discovered that others in the town were already eager to help, and finally, as the result of a meeting convened by the Mayor on 13th December 1938, the Reading (now Reading and District) Refugee Committee came into being.

As I knew German and was familiar with the background of the refugees, I accepted, temporarily, until someone else could be found for the job, the office of Organising Honorary Secretary of the Committee, little supposing at the time that this would gradually develop into my main business. But so it has come about, and if at first I sometimes felt the desire to do something more obviously useful to the country and for the war effort, I comforted myself by

---

78 William Ewart Clarke McIlroy was the owner of McIlroy's department store in Reading and mayor of the town 1938–43.

remembering that the Home Office sent a special message to the first general conference of Refugee Societies in 1939 saying that Government considered their work of first-rate national importance.

Of its intrinsic value there can be no doubt in the minds of any who have been privileged to take an active share in it. But as there still appears to be some confusion among the general public it may be wise to set down exactly the type of foreigner the Refugee Societies, collaborating with the Central Committee at Bloomsbury House, London, set out to assist. This country has been able to shelter many governments and individuals whose homelands have been overrun by the enemy, and all these deserve every bit of help and sympathy that can be given them in their misfortunes. But it is not with the ordinary French, Belgians, Dutch, Poles, Czechs, Norwegians, Luxembourgers and the rest that the Refugee Committees, specifically so-called, are primarily concerned. Their clients are mainly those refugees from Nazi oppression who, because of their political and cultural activities, their religious creeds, or for most of them, their Jewish blood, have been rendered stateless and subjected to the horrors of the concentration camp or of Hitler's extermination policy. For the most part German-speaking, and, until 1933, feeling themselves to be citizens of the lands in which they grew up and where their ancestors had lived for many centuries, these people are here stigmatised as 'enemy aliens', though with every reason to hate and oppose the 'enemy' with whom they are only too often confused because of their origin and mother tongue.

As is now well known, from the moment when Hitler came into power he began to put into practice his theories of racial discrimination and to carry out his policy of systematic extermination. To begin with the Jews were ostracised, deprived of civil rights, of property, of permission to work. During this first period a certain proportion of them were enabled to leave their homes and to flee to such lands as consented to admit them, after 1937 penniless, either in transit to other countries for which they had obtained visas, or permanently. These permits to escape were granted by the Nazis only after extreme procrastination, extortion and maddening delay. They were obtainable almost only by the wealthy and influential and were quite beyond the reach of the Jewish masses. Visas for other countries were almost equally hard to procure. For the great majority the position became increasingly hopeless until finally several millions of these wretched people were done to death by a variety of unspeakable torments – in concentration camps, by starvation, by gas, burning by steam, burning in closed buildings, mass electrocution, mass shooting and by the 'death trains', in which, herded together in hermetically sealed trucks, men, women, and children were slowly poisoned by chlorine gas as they stood on chemically active chloride of lime which burned their feet to the bone.

These things cannot be dismissed as 'atrocity stories': every detail is vouched for by numerous eye-witnesses, and the revolting horrors must be accepted as literal facts. As Thomas Mann put it, 'Other races at the mercy of Nazi ruthlessness face humiliation, demoralisation, reduction, emasculation, slavery. For the Jews it is plain extermination that has been decided upon.' 'It is our aim' said Goebbels over the wireless, 'to exterminate the Jews. Whether we win or are defeated, we must and will reach this aim. Should the German armies be forced to retreat, they shall on their way wipe the last Jew off the earth'. And be it remembered, a Jew to the Nazi *Herrenvolk* was anyone who had a single Jewish grandparent; the fact that he was a Christian by profession and faith and that he belonged to an old-established Christian family did not save him from the effects of the blot on his scutcheon. As far as they could, the Nazis carried out their purpose: of the many millions, only a few hundred thousand European Jews survive the terror, now that the holocaust has come to an end.

At first in driblets, then up to the time of the outbreak of war in larger numbers, refugees from Nazi oppression were admitted into this country under strictly regulated conditions. Of these, some 10,000 were children who were received provided that guarantors could be found for them who would undertake to pay all necessary expenses until they attained their sixteenth birthday. These children were of all ages, and I am referring now only to those 'unaccompanied' young folk who had been sent away from home and parents in order to give them a chance of decent upbringing in friendly surroundings. Big boys of fourteen and fifteen in imminent danger from the Gestapo were the first care of the Refugee Children's Movement, but down to babies of three years old these hapless little ones were brought over in 'children's transports' and settled in friendly families, in camps and schools, and in agricultural training places. One may read in detail of the horrors many of them had already experienced in their native land over and above the separation from their families.[*]

I speak only of what I know at first-hand: for instance of the little Czech boy of four whose experiences may be deduced from the fact that he would not knowingly wear any of the clothes he brought with him; or of the big lad who took to his heels when a fellow farm labourer shouted something to him when they were at work together; or of the generally-shown terror of their school-mates and teachers;

---

[*] See, for example, E.O. Lorimer, *What Hitler Wants*, Penguin Special (1939) and F. Lafitte, *The Extermination of Aliens*, Penguin Special (1940).

or of the wonder expressed when they could 'eat as much as they liked at every meal', as one child put it to me. Or there was the pathetic little girl of seven who travelled with a younger brother of three and whose two older sisters were already at school here. Her mother, unable herself to get a visa, wrote that the child remembered her father's murder at Dachau and the receipt of his ashes as the announcement of his death. Separated from her mother and older sisters, if she were also to be placed somewhere apart from the little brother, the mother feared the child would lose her reason. Happily kind guardians were found to take them both. The mother, it has since been heard, has gone on 'a long journey' – i.e. doubtless been transported to a death camp in Poland.

It is a constant surprise that the great majority of these youngsters have developed normally into decent citizens, though it cannot be marvelled at that some of them show psychological maladjustments which require expert treatment. The deprivation of the sense of security which is one of childhood's most urgent needs, and the loss of home surroundings and parental affection, sufficiently account for the comparatively few unsatisfactory cases. The miracle is rather in the magnificent response of most to the opportunities secured for them. Numbers of young women who came here as children are at work as nursery nurses; several are probationers in hospitals or have qualified as State Registered Nurses; others have taken up various forms of social work. But the majority of both boys and girls have either been in the Forces or making munitions. Of the many soldiers among my alien friends, I mention only the LT. PERRY who shot and captured Joyce,[79] and the men who served in the Commandos and with the airborne troops. Here are one or two examples from my own young charges.

79 William Joyce, known as Lord Haw-Haw, was notorious for broadcasting German propaganda against Britain during World War II.

A Czech boy admitted to Reading University obtained first class honours in General Science and is now doing research work for the Air Ministry. Several Germans and Austrians, of both sexes, have obtained horticultural and agricultural degrees and are working on the land in various responsible positions, not to mention the many individuals who have taken up such work without previous academic training. In September 1943 a young Austrian of twenty came to ask my help in fulfilling his ambition to become a veterinary surgeon. He had arrived in this country at the age of 14½ and therefore, being over compulsory school age, had been sent straight to farm work and refused permission by the Movement for the Care of Children[80] to continue his education. Released from internment two years later, another committee forced him to take up tailoring. Without any encouragement or help, he had attended evening classes and in six months succeeded in passing his London matriculation. Then he offered his services free at weekends and on half holidays to a leading veterinary surgeon in the town where he lived, who found him so promising that a post in London was secured for him as a full time veterinary assistant, which released him from his hated job as a tailor. His new employer, equally impressed by his ability, assisted him to cover his first term's maintenance expenses at the Royal Veterinary College, evacuated to Reading, and the youth himself managed to raise his fees for the first of the five necessary sessions at the College. He has now passed his first three public examinations with distinction, and I am happy to say we have been able to obtain a free place for him for the rest of his course and have already raised sufficient money

---

80 A non-denominational organisation made up of various Jewish, Quaker and other non-Jewish groups working on behalf of refugees. Later known as the Refugee Children's Movement (RCM), it was responsible for organising the *Kindertransport*.

to secure his maintenance. Another boy, then just eighteen, we helped to get his release from agricultural work because he didn't 'think that milking cows should be a fellow's war job who had lost parents and home through the Nazis, while other men were risking their lives on battlefields, so that he could stay free'. He enlisted at once.

The adults who were allowed to land in England before the war fall into different categories. Over ten thousand people were admitted to this country as transmigrants, i.e. they had definite plans and permission for emigration elsewhere, within the next two years – for the most part to the USA or to Palestine. About half of these succeeded in re-emigrating before April 1940 and a certain number have sailed since that date. Now that transport is less difficult, from time to time individuals succeed in obtaining berths and the necessary papers, but they form a small minority. Most refugees who have been here seven years or longer have no wish to be uprooted again and cast forth to start life once more among strangers in a strange land. Only those still wish to go who have near relatives overseas. In addition to these original transmigrants, there are some forty-five thousand adult German and Austrian refugees in this country, about 75 per cent or more of whom are of Jewish origin. There are also a certain number of Russians, Poles, Czechs and Hungarians who are refugees for the same reason. But even when the great pogrom was taking place in Germany and Austria in the early part of 1939, our Government adhered to the policy of 'individual infiltration', and only those were admitted who succeeded in obtaining British visas (which often took as long as six months to secure) and also the promise of maintenance from some voluntary organisation. Many women were granted visas with permission to work as domestic servants; a certain number of married couples were allowed entry in the same capacity; a proportion of young people between the ages of sixteen and thirty-five were admitted as trainees, but, like the children, with the idea of subsequent re-emigration; some three thousand old folk over the age of sixty also gained entry and, finally, a small number of men were admitted on condition they undertook no employment, paid or unpaid.

All these immigrants were received on the explicit undertaking that they should not become a charge upon public funds,* and it is difficult to speak with adequate admiration of the generosity of those who contributed, and still contribute, to their support. From quite humble folk who 'guaranteed' a child and undertook to receive it into their home until its sixteenth year, to the well-to-do and wealthy, people of all classes opened their hearts and their purses, especially to the young.

There are schools the heads of which have received as many as six pupils free as boarders: principals and staffs

---

* Since 1941, Government has taken financial responsibility for 75 per cent of the approved administrative expenses of refugee organisations and for payment of Assistance Board allowances to individuals who required them. This step had become imperative since private charity could no longer meet the continual cost unaided now that the expected re-emigration had proved impossible as a result of war conditions. The generosity of the Government was and is deeply appreciated by all concerned, and I should like to testify from my own experience to the kindness and patience shown by all officials, national and local, with whom my work has brought me in contact in this connection. The Home Office authorities, officials of the Ministry of Labour and of the Assistance Board, local Relieving Officers, medical men, etc. – one and all have accepted their several responsibilities for refugee guests in a way which deserves public recognition. It has been exceptional for any foreigners in need of assistance to meet with anything but consideration from those to whom they had to turn. Nor must the good offices of the police be omitted in any record, for these, more than anything else, have surprised and received recognition from the refugee outlaws themselves.

have united to maintain and clothe and teach them; there is scarcely a university in the country which has not given free places to refugee students; there are many firms which have welcomed trainees to their businesses. In the welter of horrors in which the whole subject is submerged, the many proofs of humanity and decent feeling stand out to cheer and comfort one. It is quite true that there have been cases of incredibly heartless and cruel employers who have taken mean advantage of helpless foreigners. It is equally true that some of these have proved difficult, unadaptable, neurotic, warped and suspicious. But eight years' work in their cause has left me with an added respect for human nature and the heights to which, on occasion, it can rise, despite indescribable sufferings – spiritual, physical and material.

About the work accomplished by the various central bodies which have devoted themselves to the business of organisation and relief, it is difficult to speak adequately. Here again, mistakes have been made through inexperience by amateur helpers overwhelmed by the magnitude of their task, and it would be easy to give examples of inefficiency and defects of various kinds. Yet the main impression that remains is not of these, however irritating, but of the amazing determination to tackle an ever-growing burden and of the very great measure of success which has ultimately been achieved.

Bloomsbury House, now for several years the centre of refugee organisations, has become the rallying point for a new kind of social service. It has collected vast sums of money (the Jewish community alone had contributed at least £7 million in cash by the middle of 1940) and has distributed these in a variety of ways on behalf of groups and individuals. It has acted as the liaison office with Government and with officials and has co-ordinated the work of all types of committee throughout the country. It has set up medical, nursing, housing and training departments and established hostels and convalescent homes; for a long time it ran a Domestic Bureau, and so forth and so on. It is impossible to estimate the amount of humanitarian effort or the value of the results achieved in spite of all kinds of discouragement. Since the conclusion of hostilities it has housed the Search Bureau which tries to trace missing people and to establish whether they survive or where they died. It has also brought over and provided for the few hundred orphan youngsters from the concentration camps who have been allowed to come temporarily to this country for 'rehabilitation'. These concentration camp boys and girls, most of whom have had six or seven years of overwork and underfeeding in horrible conditions with no training, moral or mental, may serve as typical examples to the inhabitants of this country of the problems which Europe has to face in regard to the millions of displaced persons, young and old, who are wandering homeless and unwanted over the continent. In the most favourable conditions it must take years to restore a normal attitude of mind to those who have suffered such unspeakable misery at the hands of their fellow creatures.

The work of the Reading and District Refugee Committee in comparison has been naturally on a very minor scale and from the beginning has been in close conjunction with that of the Central Committees. For example, we never attempted ourselves to bring refugees into the country, though we often asked for arrangements to be made for the escape of individuals. Nor have we ever dealt with such matters as re-emigration, and we constantly refer to Bloomsbury House for help in the solution of particular problems. Yet with a live register varying between 600 and 1000 cases there has been ample scope for every variety of friendship, advice and help. From pre-natal care to burial, demands are made upon us, and it is no exaggeration to affirm that we have had on occasion to deal with every contingency, major crimes and murder alone excepted, that can affect human beings from birth to death.

We have throughout done our best to avoid thinking of our alien guests as 'cases', and endeavoured to deal with them as individuals and friends. The result for ourselves has been an immense widening of experience and growth of understanding and, we believe, of power to help. It is a real satisfaction to know that our office has come to be looked upon by so many as a place where sympathy may always be found even when no tangible help can be given. Our subscription lists testify to the way in which many of our clients endeavour to give proof of their gratitude for the assistance they have received and would like to pass on to others when their circumstances permit.

One recent example may be cited of a gift which was in return for no help of ours. A man and wife, well-to-do middle class people in their own country, escaped here with a domestic permit in 1939 and are still in their original situation. Their only child, a girl of sixteen, was already in Holland, preparing herself for emigration to the Holy Land. When the Nazis went into Holland they of course introduced their anti-Jewish extermination policy. The girl was interned, and her grandmother and uncle, who were with her, were eventually done to death. Pitiful appeals for help reached her parents through the Red Cross and after that there was a long and agonising silence. At last the mother came to tell me she had that morning heard that the girl – now 22 – had somehow escaped and *walked* from Holland over the Pyrenees and was safe in Spain. As the mother left my office she pressed a pound note into my hand as a thank-offering. Permission for the girl to rejoin her parents here was refused, but at least she is alive and has gained admission to Palestine where one day they may be able to meet her.

Among our earliest enterprises in Reading was the establishment of a hostel for ten or twelve youths for whom jobs as trainees were found in the town. When all these lads and their warden were interned during the panic in 1940, the hostel was transformed into a home for girls and women and carried on under the guidance of the ex-warden's wife. It is still maintained under other wardens and is one of our most important and successful bits of work, affording as it does, under their guidance, a real home and something approaching family life for the residents.

In close connection with the Committee, a Refugee Club was run by a member of the Society of Friends. This Club has proved of immense value as a meeting and recreation place and was very popular with people who came to it from all over the county. Regular English classes, concerts, lectures, debates and social events were held, and it would be difficult to exaggerate the good work that it accomplished. Correspondents of the Committee in other places in Berkshire carried on smaller clubs on the same lines, to the great benefit of all concerned. These clubs are now no longer needed since the former members have gradually become assimilated into the ordinary life of the community. But in Reading they foregather from time to time so as to keep in touch with one another.

As organising officer I have naturally found plenty to do in all these directions and in many others which need not be discussed. But there is one allied piece of work which requires mention. In 1939, the Government set up Tribunals all over the country to examine 'enemy aliens' who had been admitted and to place them in various categories, i.e. refugees from Nazi oppression, or non-refugees, classes A, B and C. Those placed in the A class were at once interned as suspects. Those marked B retained their liberty but were severely restricted in their movements. They could not, for

example, travel more than five miles without express permission from the police. Those in the C class were exempt
from restrictions except those, such as registration with the
police, which applied to all foreigners. The Tribunals consisted of a President, who was usually an eminent lawyer or
legal expert, and the local chief constable (or more usually
his representative who was the police officer responsible
for aliens in the district). It was the function of the latter to
produce the dossier of each individual who was examined.
In addition, the Refugee Committees were empowered to
appoint a Liaison Officer to act as interpreter when necessary and to produce all the additional information available
to those in personal touch with the aliens concerned. In all
there were 120 tribunals and they examined some 73,400
refugees of German and Austrian birth, including those
who had been made stateless. (About 1000 in all were, for
special reasons, such as illness, not examined.) Of these,
760 were at once interned because of serious doubts about
their *bona fides*. Of this number, only 130 men and 30 women
were classified as 'refugees from Nazi Oppression'. The tribunals for Berkshire and for Reading, of which alone I have
first-hand knowledge because I acted as one of the Liaison
Officers, treated the refugees with unfailing courtesy, patience and sympathy, though they tended to be frightened
and occasionally hysterical, especially those who had experienced previous 'examinations' by the Gestapo or who had
suffered in concentration camps. They also often forgot
their English in the stress of the moment and thereby added
to the length and difficulty of the examination. Moreover,
presidents of the Tribunals were not selected because of
their knowledge of German conditions, or of Hitler's policy:
at least one of the gentlemen in question, when first appointed, knew nothing or less than nothing of the treatment

of the Jews and of the Nuremberg Edicts.[81] He was filled with suspicion if one of the refugees who had arrived in 1933 or -4 had managed to escape with some of his money; a partnership in a neutral or allied country which produced an income was another cause of doubt, etc. Ignorance, if not prejudice, resulted in misjudgement, particularly if the manner or manners of the examinee were displeasing.

Much more serious was the lack of precision in the Home Office regulations, so that the discrepancies of treatment were very marked between various Presidents. The B class was intended (and eventually used) for doubtful cases whose records justified neither internment nor total exemption from restrictions. One of my presiding officers for the first month of the sittings placed all farm labourers, servants and schoolboys (unless in cricket or football teams) in Class B because he thought it good for them to be kept close to their work. He did the same to a Roman Catholic priest who was a master at a public school. At one sitting he placed nineteen out of twenty refugees in Class B. The next day the numbers were exactly reversed: nineteen out of twenty being placed in Class C, when a different President was in the judgement seat.

Again, the first man began by limiting the term 'refugee from Nazi Oppression' to those who had actually suffered physical ill-treatment. One result of this misapprehension was that all children who had been sent over through the

81 Properly known as the Nuremberg Laws, they were introduced on 15 September 1935 by the Reichstag at a special meeting of the Nazi Party. They forbade marriages and extramarital intercourse between Jews and Germans and the employment of German females under 45 in Jewish households, and declared that only those of German or related blood were eligible to be Reich citizens; the remainder were classed as state subjects, without citizenship rights.

Refugee Children's Movement or who had accompanied their parents were deprived of the benefit of the status; however that particular blunder was soon rectified. The other was much more serious in its effects, for when the internment policy followed a few months later, all Class B men and women were interned when the re-classification tribunals had only just got to work.

Ultimately all men, whatever their category, were interned. But this did not ever apply to the women and, unless for special reasons in individual cases, only the B women suffered this final misery. Consequently a number of perfectly reliable and respectable women spent weeks or even months in Holloway prison because the women's internment camps were not even nominally ready for their reception. (Later the Dutch and other friendly alien women refugees were also sent to Holloway when their countries were invaded and they escaped here without previous vetting by the authorities.) Nor, for that matter, were the men's camps ready either, and they were put meanwhile in totally unfit and terrible places: disused factories, derelict houses, overcrowded tents, unfurnished quarters in some respects far worse even than prisons, which at any rate provided a roof, some sort of furniture, bedding, food and medical appliances; nor do they herd convicts indiscriminately together as the unfortunate refugees were herded. Old men between sixty-five and seventy, invalids in all stages of disease, schoolboys, professional men, distinguished scientists and artists were lumped together without sanitary arrangements, adequate means of washing (eighteen taps for 2000 people at Warth Mills Camp!),[82] chairs or beds. Men who had actively opposed the Hitler régime and Jews were

---

82 For more information about conditions at Warth Mills see
    http://aircrashsites.co.uk/history/warth-mills-internment-camp

confined at close quarters with Nazis, and the ignorant army authorities treated them all as civilian enemy prisoners of war, including those whose records were well known. Moreover, internees were deprived of their identity papers and their personal possessions, which frequently disappeared altogether; nor were records kept of the inmates of the camps so that the whereabouts of individuals were unknown to the authority. They were not allowed any news and lived in the constant terror of a successful Nazi invasion. Letters did not arrive for weeks, nor were they at first allowed to communicate with their friends. And finally, hundreds were transported, many of them against their will and without farewells to their families, to Canada and Australia – numbers to perish *en route* by enemy action.

Meanwhile the anxiety and misery of the families left behind can be imagined without detailed description. Our Refugee Office was besieged by miserable women whose fears it was impossible to allay: in addition there were all kinds of business matters with which to cope – irate landlords, unpaid rent, broken agreements, furniture to store, maintenance to provide. Those were weeks of nightmare even to us who were not personally concerned. To the refugees who had come here as invited guests to find security, they must have been veritable hell. I quote from the second annual report of the Reading and District Refugee Committee, but its experiences were typical of all the case-working committees:

> Not all these people behaved with the calm self-restraint which would doubtless have mitigated their troubles. But the hysterical and overwrought must be forgiven when we remember what they had undergone in their own lands before they arrived in what they believed to be the safety of this country. Early morning removal in police vehicles naturally connoted to them the horrors of a concentration

camp and the subsequent lack of news and difficulties of correspondence augmented their fears. Thus there have been most regrettable results – attempted suicides, necessary certifications as lunatics, complete and partial breakdowns – all of which have thrown very painful responsibilities on the Committee ... not to mention the endless demands for sympathetic help, for appeals for release and for a thousand and one kinds of assistance which it is impossible to detail.

The whole business is a revolting instance of panic and loss of self-control and common sense which one would previously have supposed impossible in this country. Necessary steps to ensure security are one thing: what actually occurred was something quite different and wholly inexcusable. It is true that when the Home Office took over from the military, some of the worst features of the internment camps were remedied. But suicides and deaths and mental breakdowns could not be atoned for by belated repentance, nor could anything alter the ill-effects of what had happened.

Official action at this period goes far to explain the deterioration that took place in the public attitude towards aliens. Naturally, popular suspicion of all foreigners was encouraged, and whereas up to May 1940 there had been almost universal sympathy with Nazi victims, there now began a widespread campaign against them. It became increasingly difficult for those who were not interned to find work and lodgings, nor has their good behaviour and anxiety to serve the Allied cause even today wiped out the results of the misguided action of the authorities. Combined with continuous Fascist anti-Semitic propaganda, the results have been and are manifest in a form of Jew-baiting hitherto unknown in this country in modern times. It is necessary in any historical account of present-day happenings to call attention to this unpleasant and dangerous fact, and to point out that those who gloss it over or connive at it are definitely playing Hitler's game and doing Goebbels's work for him now that they are no more. 'The evil that men do lives after them': the growth of anti-Semitism in Britain is one very definite result of the war to end the racial discrimination taught by the Nazis.

Slowly and gradually the internment policy was reversed and the internees were released – not, as might have been expected, in accordance with their several degrees of known reliability, but in order of their supposed utility to national purposes. Thus those who could be induced to enlist in the Pioneer Corps – in non-combatant, special alien companies – were the earliest to secure their freedom. This method resulted, among other things, in the long retention of the elderly and physically unfit, and often of some of the most deserving and loyal persons who could not be brought under the White Paper categories. However, by the end of 1941 most of the internees in whom we were specially interested had regained their freedom; by that date also the general ban upon employment had been lifted, and most men and women were able to find means of supporting themselves, though generally at that time by various forms of unskilled labour.

At long last, by 1944, refugees from Nazi oppression were permitted to enlist in practically all sections of the army and ATS [Auxiliary Territorial Service], though only rarely in other branches of HM Armed Forces: they were allowed to join the various Civil Defence services and they are encouraged to take up munition work. The response was immediate and widespread and provided ample evidence of their desire to play an honourable and active part in the war against the aggressor. Some 95 per cent of the 56,000 adult 'alien enemies' in this country who were able-bodied directly contributed to the war effort in one way or another: in the Forces, in munition work, in science, engineering, industry and agriculture. Others were distinguished scholars, musicians and artists. It may safely be asserted that the alien immigrant of today is contributing at least as much to the land of his sojourn as the Flemings in the twelfth and the Huguenots and the Dutch in the seventeenth and eighteenth centuries respectively.

No decision has so far been announced by Government concerning the treatment of these people after the war. It is quite certain that only a tiny minority of those from Germany, and perhaps a slightly larger number from Austria, will wish to return to their native land. Practically no Jews will desire to do so. Except those who have near relatives overseas, the vast majority will wish to become naturalised British subjects and to remain in this country. No-one who knows and works among them can doubt the misery that will ensue if the fiat for their removal is pronounced by the authorities. Such an edict would certainly be the result of base fears over the effects on our fellow countrymen of the presence of so many competitors in the labour market.

It is therefore worthwhile to emphasise what is now generally accepted by economists as a fact: every individual living in a land, however occupied, necessarily provides work for countless persons in the satisfaction of his demands for food, clothing, housing, etc. Similarly, every fully employed and properly remunerated worker necessarily contributes to the welfare of the society of which he is a member. In addition, many of these refugees are already employing much British labour in industries – some of them first introduced by them into this country – and in agriculture; many among them are outstanding scientists, distinguished in their professions and in the arts. From the selfish point of view, Britain stands to gain much more than she could possibly lose by acting generously in her treatment of her alien guests. Finally, since there is so much fear at this time of a declining population with a preponderance of the eldest age groups, it seems foolish to banish a number of men and women, many of the younger of whom have spent most of their lives in this country and have come to feel themselves in all essentials English.

In any case there is no doubt that the various Refugee Committees will have an important part to play after the war as well as during the remaining months of hostilities, by contributing to the just solution of the many problems that must arise. What is indisputable is that the rehabilitation of Europe and the winning of a lasting peace must depend to a very large extent upon the right and humane treatment of minorities, whether at home or abroad.

Epilogue

It seems improbable that, at my age, I shall have anything further of general interest to record about my doings, so the time has come to bring these brief reminiscences to a close.

I have confined myself as far as might be to my active life, to the exclusion of the purely personal. But since the account of my work must necessarily reflect my personality, it is right to add that I have said little or nothing of what has been and remains the most important of my interests. Primarily my life has been devoted to scholarly pursuits and to the study of literature. I have keenly enjoyed many things – out-of-door activities, long tramps in the country, boating, swimming, various games and forms of athletics. I have welcomed intercourse with all sort and conditions of men, women and children and delighted in the give and take of conversation, while travel at home and abroad has given me many happy holidays. But always the stable background has been that of books, which have exerted the most enduring influence upon my life and which have been my most stimulating guides and companions. I have proved for myself the truth of Wordsworth's dictum that

> Round these, with tendrils strong as flesh and blood
> Our pastime and our happiness will grow.
> —W. Wordsworth, *Personal Talk*

Consequently it is fitting that I should conclude these rambling reminiscences of my activities with an expression of gratitude to those who awakened in me the love of learning and taught me how to appreciate the things of the mind. As, one by one, friends are taken and advancing years render my companionship less congenial to those who remain, it may be that my dependence on the fellowship of books will become more complete. Yet it is true that, even in the heyday of life and vigour, I have always consciously valued it as the most abiding happiness. Nor have I ever wavered in the ambition to add something, however little, to the sum total of knowledge. In the words of Chaucer, 'Ther is namore to seyn'.

Biographical notes

Morley mentions very many people in her memoir; some have been given brief explanations in footnotes. The list of brief biographical notes below concentrates on those people who shared Morley's concerns: Fabians, feminists, academics and those connected with Reading University. Very famous people have been omitted, as have those about whom I could find nothing significant, and those about whom Morley tells us enough in her text not to need further explanation. In one or two cases of very famous people, I have limited the notes to their social concerns.

Acronyms and initialisms of the following organisations are mentioned in these notes:

BFUW   British Federation of University Women
DNB   Oxford Dictionary of National biography
IFUW   International Federation of University Women
ILP   Independent Labour Party
LCC   London County Council
LSE   London School of Economics
NUWSS   National Union of Women Suffrage Societies
WAAC   Women's Army Auxiliary Corps
WEA   Workers' Educational Association
WRAF   Women's Royal Air Force
WSPU   Women's Social and Political Union

ALLEN, (REGINALD) CLIFFORD, 1889–1939, Fabian, politician and peace campaigner. Allen was an active Fabian and a conscientious objector, and he was variously Treasurer and Chairman of the London branch of the ILP. He was heavily involved in the emergence of a Labour newspaper, the *Daily Citizen*.

ATKINSON, MABEL, 1876–1958, suffragette and social reformer. She worked in London as a WEA tutor and also lectured in Economics at King's College. Fiercely political, she was active both as a feminist and socialist. She was a member of the Fabian Executive Committee and Education Secretary to their Summer School, which she had suggested.

BARNETT, SAMUEL AUGUSTUS, 1844–1913, Church of England clergyman and social reformer. He and his wife were responsible for the founding of Toynbee Hall, the university settlement in Whitechapel. He was an advocate of educational reforms, poor relief measures and universal pensions. He later became Canon and Sub-Dean of Westminster.

BEALE, DOROTHEA, 1831–1906, suffragist and educational reformer. She was Vice-President of the Central Society for Women's Suffrage. In 1858 she was appointed headmistress of Cheltenham Ladies' College and, through providing a more academic education, turned it into one of the most highly regarded schools in the country. With her friend and colleague Miss Buss she was the subject of a rhyme supposedly recited by schoolgirls:

> Miss Buss and Miss Beale
> Cupid's darts do not feel.
> How different from us,
> Miss Beale and Miss Buss.

BRADLEY, ANDREW CECIL, 1851–1935, literary scholar. His major work was *Shakespearean Tragedy* (1904). In 1901 he was elected to the Oxford Professorship of Poetry. He was a supporter of female suffrage, education for women and the WEA. He was 'father and moving spirit' of the English Association.

BUSS, FRANCES, 1827–94, suffragist and pioneer of education for girls. She established the North London Collegiate School for Girls, of which she was headmistress for 40 years. She was one of the leading authorities on the education of girls and believed in the importance of examinations, and of educating girls to as high a standard as boys. In 1865 she joined with Emily Davies, Dorothea Beale and other suffragists to form a women's discussion group called the Kensington Society. The following year the group formed the London Suffrage Committee and began organising a petition asking Parliament to grant women the vote.

CHAMBERS, RAYMOND WILSON, 1874–1942, literary scholar. He was a lecturer and librarian at University College, where he knew A.E. Housman and W.P. Ker. He became Professor of English Language and Literature in 1922, was President of the Philological Society in 1933 and Honorary Director of the Early English Text Society.

CLAPHAM, LILIAN, *c*.1871–1935, civil servant. She worked at the Women's University Settlement at Southwark. As a civil servant she was involved in the setting up of the women's side of employment exchanges. In 1917 she was seconded from the Ministry of Labour to be Principal Officer, Women's Section of National Service Department. She was captain of the English hockey team and a close friend of Virginia Gildersleeve (q.v.) and Caroline Spurgeon (q.v.).

CULLIS, WINIFRED CLARA, 1875–1956, educationist and physiologist. She was the first woman professor in a British medical school. She was a co-founder of the BFUW and the IFUW and was President of each 1925–9 and 1929–32 respectively.

DAVIES, ALBERT EMIL, 1875–1950, British writer, lecturer and prominent Labour Party member of the LCC, which he chaired 1940–1. He edited the *New Statesman* from 1913–31. A prominent and very active member of the Fabian Society, his particular interests were in housing, education, open spaces and transport.

DODD, FREDERICK LAWSON, 1868–1936, Fabian. He was Society Treasurer and author of various pamphlets, including *A national medical service* and *Municipal milk and public health.*

DRAKE, BARBARA [*née* Meinertzhagen], 1876–1973, political activist and author. She was a leading member of the Fabian Women's Group from 1913 and researched and wrote on women's employment, publishing *Women in Trade Unions* (1920). In 1925 she was co-opted onto the Education Committee of the LCC and is known particularly for introducing milk into all London schools in 1946.

DYSON, HENRY VICTOR, 1896–1975, academic. He taught English at the University of Reading 1924–45, when he obtained a fellowship at Merton College Oxford. He was a member of the Inklings, an informal literary discussion group that included Tolkien and C.S. Lewis. He gave several popular TV talks on Shakespeare and appeared in the film *Darling* (1965).

ENSOR, ROBERT CHARLES KIRKWOOD, 1877–1958, Fabian, journalist and historian. In 1909 he served on the national administrative council of the ILP. He was on the Executive Committee of the Fabian Society 1907–11 and 1912–19 and a member of the LCC 1910–13. He was the author of *England, 1870–1914* in the Oxford History of England series.

FAIRFIELD, JOSEPHINE LETITIA DENNY, 1885–1978, doctor and suffragist. She qualified in 1907 from Edinburgh and worked most of her life for the LCC in a broad range of public health activities, particularly relating to children's and women's health. A member of the Fabian Society and the WSPU, she was an energetic campaigner. During World War I she was medical officer to the WAAF and in 1918 became Chief Medical Officer to the new WRAF. In World War II, like Morley, she helped refugees from Nazi Germany.

FAITHFULL, LILLIAN, 1865–1952, educationist. She was Vice-Principal at King's College, Ladies Department, 1894–1907, where she promoted courses of study leading to academic qualifications. After the death of Miss Beale (q.v.) in 1906, she accepted the post of headmistress of Cheltenham Ladies College, where she worked until her retirement in 1922. She became a JP for Cheltenham, one of the first women magistrates to be appointed in England, and was particularly interested in penal reform. In her retirement she worked to provide better conditions for the poor of Shoreditch.

FAWCETT, DAME MILLICENT GARRETT [*née* Garrett], 1847–1929, educational reformer and suffragist. Sister of Elizabeth Garrett Anderson (q.v.), she was a founder of Newnham College, Cambridge, and of the NUWSS. She worked throughout her life, as speaker and writer, to further the cause of women.

FURNIVALL, FREDERICK JAMES, 1825–1910, textual scholar and editor. In 1853 he became Honorary Secretary of the Philological Society, in which role he laid the foundations for the Oxford English Dictionary. He was also the founder of a series of literary and philological societies, including the Early English Text Society (1864), the Chaucer Society and the Shelley Society (1885).

GARRETT ANDERSON, ELIZABETH, 1836–1917, physician. After considerable difficulties in finding training opportunities, Anderson finally was able to qualify and start practising in London. In 1866 she set up the St Mary's Dispensary for Women and Children and also a fund to enable poor women to use her services. She opened the New Hospital for Women in 1871 and campaigned for women to be allowed to enter the medical profession. She was on the council and the teaching staff of the London School of Medicine for Women when it opened in 1874. In 1902 she retired to Aldeburgh, where she was elected the first woman mayor in England in 1908 (until 1910). Between 1908 and 1911, she actively supported the WSPU, but later she renounced militancy, preferring the suffragist approach of her sister Millicent Fawcett (q.v.).

GILDERSLEEVE, VIRGINIA CROCHERON, 1877–1965, American educationist. Founder of the IFUW and Dean of Barnard College (which was affiliated with Columbia University), she was a strong supporter of women's rights, an early and strong supporter of the League of Nations, and after World War II, a strong anti-Zionist. She was a close friend of Caroline Spurgeon (q.v.) and Lilian Clapham (q.v.).

GOLLANCZ, SIR ISRAEL, 1863–1930, literary scholar. In 1903 Gollancz was appointed to the chair of English Language and Literature at King's College, London. He was Honorary Director of the Early English Text Society, President of the Philological Society, chairman of the Shakespeare Association, and one of the founders and first Secretary of the British Academy.

GWYNNE VAUGHAN, DAME HELEN CHARLOTTE ISABELLA [*née* Fraser], 1879–1967, mycologist, botanist and women's activist. One of the first women students at King's College, she became head of the Botany Department at Birkbeck in 1909. Alongside teaching she worked in girls' clubs and supported the suffragists. In 1917 she was appointed chief controller of the WAAC, stationed in France; and in 1918 she became head of the WRAF. In 1919 she was made a DBE.

HANKINSON, MARY, 1868–1952, gymnastics teacher and Fabian. She was an active organiser of the Fabian Summer Schools where she was responsible for the musical and theatrical evenings, the outdoor activities such as walking, country dancing and Swedish drill before breakfast, and the domestic arrangements. Shaw claimed that she was the model for St Joan.

HENDERSON, ARTHUR, 1863–1935, Scottish Labour politician. He was several times chairman of the Labour Party and a successful Foreign Secretary 1929–31. A crusader for disarmament, he was awarded the 1934 Nobel Peace Prize and helped to establish the League of Nations.

HERFORD, CHARLES HAROLD, 1853–1931, academic. He was a literary scholar and external examiner at King's College, London. He taught at Aberystwyth and Manchester, and though his chair was in English Language and Literature, he was well versed in several European languages. His interests extended to the German Romantics, Dante, Wordsworth, Goethe and Browning. He wrote for the Manchester Guardian and in 1927 published *The Post-war Mind of Germany, and other European Essays.*

KOCK-LINDBERG, KARIN [*née* Kock], 1891–1976, Swedish social democrat politician and economist. She was a lecturer at Stockholm University 1933–8 and became Professor of Economics in 1945. She worked as economic adviser at the Women's Workers Association in 1936 and was a government delegate at the International Workers' Conference in Paris in 1945. She served as Minister for the Domestic Economy in 1948–9, the first female Minister in Sweden, and was also Vice-President of the IFUW.

LAWRENCE, ARABELLA SUSAN, 1871–1947, politician. Originally a Conservative, she changed her politics in the belief that state action was essential for social improvement. She joined the Fabian Society, serving on its Executive 1913–45, and developed close friendships with Sidney and Beatrice Webb. Strongly involved in women's trade unionism, as MP for East Ham North she became one of the first three female Labour MPs. In 1918 Lawrence was elected to the new women's section of the party's National Executive, and in October 1930 she became the first woman to chair the Labour Party conference.

LOYD-LINDSAY, HARRIET SARAH, LADY WANTAGE [*née* Jones-Loyd], 1837–1920, benefactor. After the death in 1901 of her husband, who had been the first President of Reading University College, she was appointed Vice-President and life Governor. She built and endowed a men's hall of residence, Wantage Hall (1908), and in 1911 gave £50,000 towards an endowment fund. The Royal Berkshire Hospital also benefited from her generosity. She was the cousin and lifelong close friend of Madeleine Shaw-Lefevre (q.v.).

MCKILLOP, MARGARET [*née* Seward], 1864–1929, scientist and university teacher. She lectured in Chemistry at King's College, Ladies Department, 1897–1912, where she was a strong supporter of the move to develop domestic science as an academic discipline. During World War I she worked in the Ministry of Food, studying nutrition and health. After the war she worked as a member of the Fabian Women's Group to improve the status of domestic work. She also published a textbook on economics, a book on food values, and, with her son, *Efficiency Methods: An introduction to scientific management* (1917).

MACKINDER, SIR HALFORD JOHN, 1861–1947, geographer and politician. At Oxford he became involved with the extension movement and lectured at several centres. One of the founders of the Geographical Association, in 1892 he was appointed first Principal of the extension college at Reading, which thrived and grew rapidly under his leadership. In 1902 Reading became a University College and Mackinder served as Principal until 1903, when he was appointed the second Director of the LSE. In later years he became an MP and was renowned for his geopolitical writings.

MACKINNON, DORIS LIVINGSTONE, 1883–1956, protozoologist. She specialised in the parasites of insects and developed a reputation as a brilliant lecturer at University College Dundee. During the war she worked in military hospitals and studied amoebic dysentery. In 1919 she was appointed lecturer in Zoology at King's College, University of London, later being promoted to Reader (1921) and Professor (1927).

MANSBRIDGE, ALBERT, 1876–1952, founder of the WEA. He had to leave school at the age of 14 but attended university extension classes at King's College, London. Concerned that the extension classes were not attracting the working classes, he founded the WEA in 1903, and within two years eight branches had been set up. In 1905 Mansbridge abandoned clerical work to become its full-time General Secretary, resigning in 1915 owing to illness. Later he went on to found several other adult education groups.

MAWER, SIR ALLEN, 1879–1942, scholar of place names and university administrator. He trained at London University and Cambridge, taught at Sheffield, Newcastle and Liverpool and returned to London University as Provost in 1930. He began a systematic survey of English place names and was instrumental in the founding of the English Place-Name Society.

MEYER, ADELE, LADY MEYER [*née* Levis], 1862/3–1930, campaigner for social reform, society hostess, opera patron and art collector. She was a suffragist and leader in social work and headed many initiatives on behalf of women: she was the first to organise cooking lessons in the home for mothers and established the first rural health centre in Britain. She was also involved in investigating the conditions of work for women in the London clothing trade. This resulted in a book: *Makers of Our Clothes: A case for trade boards, being the results of a year's investigation into the work of women in London in the tailoring, dressmaking and underclothing trades* (1909).

MORRIS, WILLIAM, 1834–96, craftsman, poet and visionary social-ist. Better known today for his work as designer and craftsman, when nearly fifty Morris joined the Social Democratic Federation, and when this was disrupted in 1884 he formed a breakaway group, the Socialist League. A skilled journalist, he funded and edited the Socialist League newspaper, *The Commonweal*. He was heavily involved in political protest in Britain in 1886 and 1887, taking part in over 100 public protest meetings. In *News from Nowhere* (1890) he imagines a utopian future in which money, 'wage slavery' and marriage have been abolished. It was one of the essential socialist texts of the early twentieth century.

OAKELEY, HILDA DIANA, 1867–1950, educationist and author. After teaching in Canada 1899–1905, she moved to King's College as lecturer in Philosophy and Vice-Principal at the Women's Department. She was well known in academic circles, a member of the Aristotelian Society, and Vice President of the BFUW from 1909 until her death. During World War I she worked as resident warden of the Passmore Edwards (later Mary Ward) Settlement, where, among other things she ran boys' clubs and 'play centres'. After the war she returned to academic life, becoming head of the Philosophy Department at King's College.

PALMER, ALFRED, 1852–1936, biscuit maker and benefactor. Second son of the co-founder of Huntley & Palmers of Reading, he was a director of Huntley & Palmers 1878–1936, President of the Council of Reading University 1926–30, and High Sheriff of Berkshire in 1905.

PALMER, GEORGE WILLIAM, 1851–1913, biscuit manufacturer and benefactor. Eldest son of the co-founder of Huntley & Palmers of Reading, he was a notable benefactor to Reading University College, serving on its Council from 1902 onwards, and as Vice-President from 1905 until his death. In addition to *ad hoc* gifts for building, he assisted in tackling its debts by making generous anonymous donations and helped to fund the College's bid for university status. In 1882 he was elected to Reading Borough Council, serving as mayor 1888–9. He was Liberal MP for Reading 1892–5, and again 1898–1904. He served as JP for both Reading and Berkshire.

PANKHURST, EMMELINE [*née* Goulden], 1858–1928, militant suffragette leader. A radical from an early age, and married to a barrister who was a strong supporter of women's suffrage, she was a member of the Fabian Society, the ILP and the Women's Franchise League. In 1903 she founded the militant WSPU. A charismatic speaker, she participated in much direct action and was frequently imprisoned and force-fed.

PEASE, EDWARD REYNOLDS, 1857–1955, Fabian. A founder member of the Fabian Society, he acted variously as paid and honorary Secretary between 1889 and 1939. Principally an administrator, he wrote the official *History of the Fabian Society* (1916) and various tracts and articles. He was the Society's representative on the Labour Party's National Executive 1900–13.

PEMBER REEVES, MAGDALEN, known as Maud, 1865–1953, Fabian. Born in New Zealand, she was involved there in the early granting of votes for women. She came to England with her husband in 1896 and soon joined the Fabian Society, the NUWSS and the Women's Liberal Association. She co-founded the Fabian Women's Group and is best known for her report *Round About a pound a Week* (1913), the result of a survey of 42 Lambeth families.

PERRY, GEOFFREY HOWARD, 1922–2014, soldier, publisher, refugee. Originally named Horst Pinschewer, he was a German Jewish boy who had been evacuated to England. Having been interned for several months as an enemy alien, when released he joined the British Army's Pioneer Corps and ended up a major. He was famous for having captured Lord Haw-Haw and became a publishing entrepreneur, prison visitor and JP.

PLUMER, ELEANOR, 1885–1967, academic. Although registered at King's College, Ladies Department, she read English at Oxford as an external student. She continued at King's College as a lecturer and tutor to women students and subsequently became Warden of the Mary Ward Settlement (1923–27) and of St Andrew's Hall in the University of Reading (1927–31). In 1940 she became Principal of the Society of Oxford Home Students, which later became St Anne's College.

POPE, MILDRED KATHERINE, 1872–1956, French scholar. She became the first woman to hold a readership at Oxford University, where she established and developed the teaching of medieval French. She was committed to social causes and an active feminist, campaigning for women's suffrage and recruiting female dons to the cause. During World War I she worked with the Friends' War Victims' Relief Expedition in northern France. Dorothy Sayers portrayed her as Miss Lydgate in *Gaudy Night*.

PRIDEAUX, SARAH TREVERBIAN, 1853–1933, bookbinder, teacher, writer and collector of fine bindings. Known particularly for *An Historical Sketch of Bookbinding* (1893), she also wrote a well-regarded history of aquatint engraving. One of the best of the women binders of the period, she also taught the craft.

RUCKER, THEREZA CHARLOTTE, LADY RUCKER [*née* Story-Maskelyne], 1863–1941, promoter of household science teaching. 'She was one of the main forces behind the establishment of a course in "home science" at King's College for Women, London, in 1908. The course became a London degree subject in 1920 and led to the establishment of King's College of Household and Social Science in 1928.' (DNB) She favoured a degree course which could train women for the new careers in social work, health visiting and institutional management which were opening up at the time, but would also be relevant to them as wives and mothers.

RUSKIN, JOHN, 1819–1900, art critic and social thinker. Ruskin was the major art critic of his day, but he was also a great teacher, campaigner and controversialist. His views on educational and social reform were hugely influential, and he was admired by, among others, Ghandi, Proust and Tolstoy. In the UK his influence, particularly on Toynbee and the Webbs, was felt in such areas as women's education, the minimum wage, child labour and environmental protection, and his thinking inspired the founders of the NHS.

RUSSELL, ALYSSA [*née* Whitall Pearsall Smith], known as Alys, 1867–1951, political activist. She worked for women's rights and sought to improve the immediate social conditions of poor women. She was the first wife of Bertrand Russell; they divorced in 1921.

SANDERS, WILLIAM STEPHEN, 1871–1941, politician and Fabian. He was a member of the Fabian Society Executive Committee, of which he was secretary 1913–20, and author of Fabian tracts on the legal minimum wage, the socialist party in Germany and the International Labour Organisation. He was MP for Battersea North 1929–31 and 1935–40.

SHAW, GEORGE BERNARD, 1856–1950, playwright and Fabian. Alongside his enormous output of plays and other theatrical work, he was an influential Fabian, serving on the Executive Committee 1884–1911; he edited *Fabian Essays* and wrote many socialist tracts. Through the Fabians, Shaw assisted at the formation of the ILP in 1893. Before the consolidation of London local government he was himself a vestryman and borough councillor for St Pancras (1897–1903). After losing an election for the LCC he turned down appeals that he run for parliamentary seats.

SHAW, MRS BERNARD *see* **TOWNSHEND, CHARLOTTE PAYNE**

SHAW-LEFEVRE, MADELEINE SEPTIMIA, 1835–1914, college head. She came late to social work, but by 1877 she was on the committee of, and an active visitor for, the Metropolitan Association for Befriending Young Servants. The council of Somerville Hall appointed her Principal in 1879 and she remained in post for a decade. During her principalship women began to be admitted to university examinations (1884).

SIBLY, SIR (THOMAS) FRANKLIN, 1883–1948, academic. He studied geology as an external candidate at London University. In 1908 he was appointed lecturer in Geology at King's College. He later taught at Cardiff, Newcastle upon Tyne and Swansea before being appointed Principal of the University of London in 1926. In 1929 he became Vice-Chancellor at the University of Reading, where he remained until 1946.

SNELL, HENRY, BARON SNELL, 1865–1944, British socialist politician and campaigner. He joined the ILP and, in 1894, the Fabian Society. He was active in supporting the Bryant and May match factory strike and the London dock strike of 1889. He became an MP in 1922 and served in government under Ramsay MacDonald and Winston Churchill, and as the Labour Party's leader in the House of Lords in the late 1930s.

SPURGEON, CAROLINE FRANCES ELEANOR, 1869–1942, English scholar. She studied English at King's College and University College, London, 1895–9, and lectured in English at Bedford College, London, from 1901. Her most famous published work was *Shakespeare's Imagery and What It Tells Us* (1935). She and Virginia Gildersleeve (q.v.), who became her lifelong companion, founded the IFUW in 1919. Spurgeon served as the organisation's President 1920–4 and also helped establish Crosby Hall.

STRACHEY, RACHEL PEARSALL CONN [*née* Costelloe], known as Ray, 1887–1940, suffragist. She studied mathematics at Newnham College, Cambridge (1905–8), where she became interested in the suffrage movement. Later she joined the London Society for Women's Suffrage. She worked closely with Millicent Fawcett and was political secretary to Nancy Astor, the first female MP. She edited *The Common Cause* and then its successor, *The Women's Leader*, and was the author of a number of books on women's suffrage.

TOWNSHEND, EMILY CAROLINE, 1849–1934, Fabian. She was a member of the Executive Committee and wrote three of their tracts, including one on William Morris and one on the case for school nurseries.

TOWNSHEND, CHARLOTTE PAYNE, 1857–1943, benefactor and Fabian. She was an Irish heiress who met Beatrice and Sidney Webb in 1895 and was involved with them in founding the LSE, which she supported generously with both time and money until her death. In 1896 she gave £1,000 towards the establishment of the library and was among its first trustees. She married George Bernard Shaw in 1898.

UNDERHILL, EVELYN MAUD BOSWORTH, 1875–1941, religious writer and spiritual director. A student at King's College, Ladies Department, she was the first woman to lecture to the clergy in the Church of England, and one of the first woman theologians to lecture in English colleges and universities. She was a prolific author and also an award-winning bookbinder, studying with the most renowned masters of the time. During World War I, she worked for the Admiralty in naval intelligence.

WANTAGE, LADY *see* **LOYD-LINDSAY, HARRIET SARAH**

WEBB, BEATRICE, 1858–1943, and **SIDNEY**, 1859–1947, social reformers and pioneers of social science in Britain. Enormously influential, they developed theories of social evolution that were founded upon analysis of underlying structures and systems and focussed on co-operation, trade unionism, collectivism, social policy and public administration. Amongst their important achievements were the foundation of the LSE, the relaunching of the Labour Party, the remodelling of London education, the invigoration of the Fabian Society and the creation of the *New Statesman*.

WILSON, CHARLOTTE MARY [*née* Martin], 1854–1944, socialist and feminist. She joined the Fabian Society and led the anarchist faction within the group. She was also a member of the English Anarchist Circle, editing and contributing to its magazine *Freedom*. She co-founded the Fabian Women's Group in 1908 and led its research into women's social and political interests, described in *Fabian Women's Group: Three years' work* (1911). During World War I she engaged in welfare work for British prisoners of war, for which she was awarded an OBE in 1919.

Index

teaching career
—King's College   76, 80–81, 87,
—Reading   97–99, 111, 114–9, 120, 121
—WEA   125–8
World War I   146–153
World War II   160–181
Morley family
grandmother   20, 23, 25, 27, 28, 29, 45, 57
house   25–28
Morley, Leah (*mother*)   15, 25, 28, 29, 30–31, 44–46, 57, 67
Morley, Alexander (*father*)   11–12, 18, 20–22, 25, 28, 36, 52, 57
—EM and independence   43–44, 47, 65, 66, 67, 76
servants   28–31
Morris, William   40n, 131, 193, 199

names, use of   94–95
Natural History Museum   13

Oakeley, Hilda   85–86, 194
Oxford English Dictionary   93
Oxford University   50, 51, 71, 75, 110, 120, 124, 127, 192
Honours Schools   49, 50, 51, 54, 78
University Extension movement   99
women and degrees   74–75n

Palmer family   102, 111, 194, 195
professorships, female   119–120
Morley's battle   115–9

Queen Victoria   23

Reading Borough   101, 105, 123
Recreation Club   151–2
Refugee Committee   162, 171–2, 173, 177

Two Rivers Press has been publishing in and about Reading since 1994.
Founded by the artist Peter Hay (1951–2003), the press continues
to delight readers, local and further afield, with its varied list of
individually designed, thought-provoking books.